The Adventurous Gardener

The Adventurous Gardener
by Nancy Wilkes Bubel

with illustrations by Barry Moser

DAVID R. GODINE, Publisher • Boston

Other Books by Nancy Wilkes Bubel
Vegetables Money Can't Buy But You Can Grow
The Seed-Starter's Handbook
Working Wood (with Michael Bubel)

David R. Godine, Publisher, Inc.
306 Dartmouth Street
Boston, Massachusetts 02116

ISBN: 0-87923-275-7 HC; 0-87923-276-5 SC.
LCC NO: 78-74251.

Parts of the chapter 'Sweet Grapes' have
appeared in 'Grapes that Delight Us Most,'
an article published in *Organic Gardening and Farming*
(September, 1973).

Printed in the United States of America

DEDICATION

To my friend Harriet Benedict Heaney,
a truly adventurous gardener who has made
an Eden out of a backyard in Philadelphia.

Contents

Foreword

Gardening is a lifelong adventure. Even a small backyard can hold a world of discovery for the gardener who is willing to try new methods and taste new foods. If you take pleasure in providing the freshest and best food for your table, in quality and variety not to be found in any store, I hope you'll find this book a helpful guide to branching out into areas you've not yet explored. If it has always seemed to you unfortunate to arbitrarily divide the vegetables from the flower garden, you'll find here that flowers have not been forgotten. And if you sometimes like to experiment just for the stimulation of trying something new, why, then I hope you'll find encouragement in these pages when the doldrums hit or when you're looking for new worlds to conquer.

This book is a potpourri of out-of-the-ordinary things to grow and ways to grow them. It is a book to dip into, to use as a guide when you're ready to take the next step in a new direction. I cannot imagine that anyone would follow everything in it in any one year. It has taken me twenty-three years of gardening to arrive at some of the modest beginnings sketched here. But, for that very reason, I would like to think that these hints might constitute a gardening companion for you that would span seasons and years and give you, each year for a good while, a nudge in a new direction.

Ever since the age of twelve I've been making lists . . . lists not only of things that must be done, but also of the extras, the spice, the little adventures I want to try. When I was twelve, my list included drawings I wanted to make, collections I wanted to start, odd items I hoped to find, crafts I intended to learn. I never did it all, of course. But I still make lists, at least mentally, of everyday adventures that have caught my imagination. When a publisher asked me for some biographical material some years ago, I included three of my ambitions at the time:

> To identify and learn to use more wild mushrooms;
> To write a book;
> To achieve more nearly the balance between work and study/
> enrichment described by Helen and Scott Nearing in their
> book *Living The Good Life.* (Our family had just spent a
> summer building a barn and I was feeling a little short on
> the study/enrichment end of things!)

Right now, if you were to ask me what is on my list, I'd say I'm still working on the mushrooms and the bread-work/study-enrichment balance, contemplating my fifth book, and hoping to write more. In addition, I'd like to try growing cultivated mushrooms and breeding iris and day lilies. I want to do much more with heirloom and unusual vegetables, especially those that can't be found in seed catalogs. I intend to establish more wildflowers here on our farm and, within the year, will have a solar greenhouse which will be the focus of many more experiments as well as a dependable incubator for winter salads and spring seedlings. Ten years from now, the list will be different . . . but I'm reasonably sure that there *will* be a list.

Consider this book, then, a suggested list of gardening adventures. . . each with some signposts from my experience, but at the same time open-ended for your further exploration.

The book is not intended to be anything like the XYZ of gardening, though. I doubt whether that book will ever be written; at least I hope it won't. I hope that there will always be more to discover . . . new plants to grow, new techniques to try, new ways to plan and plant. You'll find here discoveries that I've enjoyed making, experiments I've found worthwhile, new angles, opportunities, challenges, and satisfactions in gardening.

Although the book goes beyond the basic ABCs of digging a garden and growing beans and tomatoes, it is written just as much for the amateur, the new gardener, as for the experienced and accomplished plant grower. My hope is that both beginning and advanced gardeners will find here some hint of new directions to try, new specialties to explore. Sources for seeds and supplies are listed at the end of this book.

If you discover something special, I'd love to hear about it. Happy gardening!

Nancy Bubel
Wellsville, Pennsylvania
1979

Acknowledgments

I'm indebted to the following people for their help in pulling this book into shape:

Judy Hu, Managing Editor, who knew what the book needed.

Jocelyn Riley, Editor, whose talent for organization has made a big difference.

David Godine, whose enthusiasm and support encouraged me.

Mary Grace Bubel, my daughter, who patiently typed the manuscript.

Other Voices

Along with the observations and directions from my experience and research, I'd like to share with you some of my favorites among the thoughts that other gardeners have expressed about the adventure of growing things. Taken together, these words might be said to form a matrix into which you can fit your discoveries as you experiment and learn. Take a moment, then, to listen to these other voices.

'The garden is forever multitudinous, multiform, overlapping, interlocking.'
    Gulielma Alsop, *April in the Branches*

'The invariable mark of wisdom is to see the miraculous in the common.'
    Ralph Waldo Emerson

'I believe it is better to share what I can than to stop sharing because I don't know all there is to know.'
    Mara Cary, *Basic Baskets*

'There's not a sprig of grass that shoots uninteresting to me.'
    Thomas Jefferson, age 43

'I'm still devoted to the garden . . . although an old man I am but a young gardener.'
    Thomas Jefferson, age 68

'I shall go on going against the rules. That is the only way one can learn.'
    V. Sackville-West, *A Joy of Gardening*

'Originally, the word (weeds) was we' ods, and it was the Anglo Saxon name for all herbs and small plants . . . to past generations of men, all plants were regarded with respect.'
    Audrey Wynne Hatfield, *How to Enjoy Your Weeds*

'No creature of the soil stands alone – all are interwoven, their pasts and futures, in the economy of a piece of earth.'
    Peter Farb, *Living Earth*

'Gardening offers a chance for man to regulate at least one aspect

of his life, to control his environment and show himself as he
wishes to be.'
    Ann Leighton, *Early American Gardens.*

'I think the richest vein is somewhere hereabouts.'
    Henry David Thoreau

'He who sows thickly gathers thinly.
He who sows thinly gathers thickly.'
    French folk saying

'God Almighty first planted a garden; and indeed, it is the purest of
human pleasures; it is the greatest refreshment to the spirits of
man; without which buildings and palaces are but gross handy-
works; and a man shall ever see that, when ages grow to civility
and elegance, man comes to build stately sooner rather than to
garden finely: as if gardening were the greater perfection.'
    Sir Francis Bacon

'All the hope of the nation was contained in those packets of seeds,
transported across the ocean or across the land at such peril,
planted with depths of emotion hard to recapture in today's
luxurious way of life.'
    Bertha P. Reppert, *A Heritage of Herbs*

'Food is our common property, the body of the world, our eating of
the world, our treasure of change and transformation, sustenance
and continuation.'
    Edward Espe Brown, *Tassajara Cooking*

'You cannot separate life into parts; all is of the Divine. . . . When
you delve deeply into anything you will find God is there.'
    The Findhorn Garden by The Findhorn Community

'One of the best things about a garden, large or small, is that it is
never finished. It is a continual experiment.'
    Margery Bianco, *Green Grows the Garden*

I. Vegetables

Growing Grandmother's Vegetables
Fall Vegetable Planting
Growing Perennial Vegetables from Seed
Sweet Potatoes Forever
Oriental Vegetables
Raising Vegetables in the Closet

Growing Grandmother's Vegetables

Cardoon

Behind the picket fences and boxwood hedges of yesterday's gardens, there were vegetables to be found that might not be recognizable to the average contemporary gardener. Some of these were staples in Grandmother's garden. Others were, even then, heirloom varieties, like the special strain of beans handed down in Grandfather's family for several generations, and maintained by faithful replanting and family legend. Still others, like rocket, were grown out of habit, and because they were dependable, rather than for any special flavor qualities.

In order to keep a vegetable heritage alive, foods must be grown to renew the seed, and harvested and cooked to be appreciated. Perhaps you'd like to grow some of these old reliables in your garden. You'll never know, until you try, what you might have been missing! Here are some popular old favorites and directions for growing and serving them.

Beans (Heirloom Beans)

Phaseolus vulgaris

Back in the days when the latest thing in kitchen appliances was a new nickel-trimmed black wood stove, shell beans and dry beans were appreciated in all their variety. A family would save and plant seed of traditional favorites from one season to another, often handing down special local strains from father to son. Some of these old beans have colorful names, and each has even now a loyal following of devotees who would plant no other kind.

Shell or horticultural beans, unlike green snap beans, are grown for the meaty seed-bean rather than the pod. In most cases, the pod of a good baking bean is tough and stringy. Some, like that of the red kidney bean, are inedible, but others, like the Wade, are tender and good as green beans too.

Shell beans are removed from the mature but still-green pod, usually in early to mid summer, and cooked like limas – by simmering for fifteen minutes – or added to soups. Some especially tender kinds like the large succulent Vermont cranberry bean may be cooked more briefly – for two to three minutes – and then buttered. Shell beans will keep in the refrigerator for a week or so but must be frozen for longer storage.

Dry beans keep well all winter – for years, in fact, as long as they are protected from animals and insects. To obtain dry beans from the same plants, let the shell beans continue to mature until the pod is brittle and the beans inside are hard and dry. Let them dry further indoors in a warm, airy place. To kill any resident insect pests, heat the beans in a 180 degree F. oven for fifteen minutes, then turn off the oven and leave the beans in it for another hour.

The dried beans are good in soups and casseroles. To savor them at their best, though, you really should make a pot of baked beans. The old New England custom of serving baked beans and cornbread for Saturday night dinner has much to recommend it. Add a tossed green salad, glasses of fresh cold milk, and you have a complete meal. The baked beans were often warmed over for breakfast the next day. And have you ever eaten a baked bean sandwich? Excellent with a touch of ketchup.

The following heirloom beans are just a sampling of the range of traditional favorites for which seed may still be obtained.

BLACK TURTLE SOUP BEAN

A tradition in the Southern states especially, but it grows well in the North, too. The plant is small and bushy and the young green pods may be eaten as snap beans. For black bean soup, though, it's outstanding.

FAVA BEANS *Vicia faba*

An ancient food crop well known to the early Romans and grown in China 5,000 years ago. They are sometimes called horse beans or broad beans. The large oblong beans are treated like shell beans – popped out of the seven- to twelve-inch-long pods and cooked in simmering water until tender. Unlike garden snap beans, favas are frost-resistant and thrive in cool weather. They are, in fact, commonly grown in England where the cool moist climate is just to their liking. Here in North America, we must plant the seed early in the spring, as soon as the ground can be worked, in order to give the favas the eighty-five days they need to grow before hot weather knocks them down. Some parts of Canada have the kind of fairly long, cool summers that fava beans like best.

Bush forms are available, but most fava bean plants have a somewhat trailing habit, growing to a height of three feet and requiring some kind of fence or string support. Plant seeds five inches apart.

It might be a good idea to make your first planting of fava beans a small one until you determine whether you are one of the few people who experience an allergic reaction after eating them.

JACOB'S CATTLE

Many families in New England, especially, couldn't keep house without this old favorite baking bean. Pick the shell beans when the plant is nine to ten weeks old or leave them on the plant to dry for a winter supply. The seed is white with spots of burgundy color – pleasing just to look at! A shelf of jars containing rosy, buff, and mottled dried beans of different sorts is one of the special visual delights of being prepared for the winter.

LOWE'S CHAMPION

Popular as shell beans, the dark reddish-purple seeds have a fine flavor. You can eat the young pods as snap beans, too. These eighteen- to twenty-four-inch tall bush beans grow well in both warm and cool climates.

SCARLET RUNNER BEANS *Phaseolus coccineus*

In many old gardens, a trellis or a plot by the back porch supported a luxuriant tapestry of scarlet runner beans. Or there might have been a bean tent – a vine-covered pole tripod – planted at the edge of the garden just for fun and decoration. The bright red flowers and large leaves are strikingly attractive. Then, as now, it was all right to plant some flowers 'just for pretty,' but the beautiful was often found to be useful as well. The pods of the scarlet runner beans I've grown were so big (twelve to fifteen inches long) and tough that I never considered eating the beans green, even when very young, although I've heard that some people do. I have it on good authority, though, that the handsome seed-beans inside the pod are good to eat fresh when they're boiled and buttered or tossed by the handful into the soup pot.

The vine of the scarlet runner bean grows to ten feet tall, so it must have some kind of support. Plant the seeds four inches apart when danger of frost is past.

SOLDIER BEANS

When I was a child growing up near Boston, you could buy soldier beans at the grocery store. Now all you can find is the small navy pea bean, the Great Northern, or the red kidney. Children like to look for the 'soldier,' a deep maroon man-shaped pattern on the hilum of each bean. Best for baking, these grow well even in cool climates.

YELLOW EYE

Prized for soup and baking, this plant yields well and adapts to varied soil and weather conditions. As you might expect, the small oval beans are favorites in New England, where there are bean-baking connoisseurs in most every town.

Cardoon
Cynara cardunculus

Cardoon had sufficient commercial importance, in the 1890s, to appear in a book written for market gardeners. This member of the large thistle family is an older cousin of the more highly refined globe artichoke. A perennial in the warm Mediterranean area where it originated, cardoon is treated as an annual in the North, where it often has the last word, nevertheless, since it self-sows readily.

Treat the young plant like a tomato plant, sowing seed indoors six to eight weeks before your frost-free date, and setting out plants about two feet apart in rows spaced three feet apart. In the rich, deeply dug soil it prefers, cardoon grows to an imposing size – four feet tall and nearly that wide, leaf-tip to leaf-tip. It resembles a large celery plant with deeply cut, slightly woolly or hairy gray-green leaves and spiny ribs along the stalks. It will grow in part shade, so you can plant it next to your tall corn. In a dry season, the stalks may turn woody and hollow-centered unless irrigated.

Cardoon is grown for the tender heart stalks and leaves which form in its center when the plant is blanched. Start in September to prepare the plant for fall eating by bunching the stalks of each clump together and wrapping newspaper around them. Fasten the paper on with string or rubber bands. Then bank soil around the stalks, almost up to the coarse top leaves of the plant, taking care not to let soil sift down into the heart of the plant.

Blanching takes four or five weeks, so sometime in October you can unwrap a plant, wash and peel the spiny strings from each stalk, and chop the stalk into one-inch pieces. The naturally bitter flavor of the cardoon will have been tempered by blanching. Simmer the vegetable until tender – about twenty minutes – and serve it with cheese sauce, spaghetti, butternut squash, or other mild, smooth contrasting food, or include one cup of the cooked cubes in your favorite casserole.

Cardoon survives the first few light frosts of fall and will last even longer if well banked with earth. True devotees go so far as to gently bend the stalks down into foot-deep trenches and mound soil over them to gain a few more weeks of the delicacy.

Chayote

Sechium edule

This wonderfully versatile perennial vine isn't, unfortunately, for everyone. It can only be grown where summers are long and hot – in the South and West – but it seems to me that it would be well worth trying in a greenhouse. Actually, you can grow chayote as an annual if you have 135 good warm (not just frost-free) days in your growing season, provided you get an early start.

The chayote has been feeding people for centuries – since the days of the Aztecs and probably even before that. There is scarcely a part of the plant that can't be used for food. The squash-like fruit – resembling a large, wrinkled green pea – is the primary food crop. It has a mild flavor and is usually cooked like summer squash. The roots, which run a close second in popularity, may be cooked and served like potatoes. The large seed inside the fruit is also good – boiled or sliced and fried. And you can even eat the young leaves. Surely someone, somewhere, has tried pickling the stems and eating the flowers! (The only chayote parts I can recommend as definitely edible, though, are the root, fruit, seed, and young leaf.)

Chayote doesn't seem to be offered by many of the seed or plant catalogs I've come across, but you shouldn't have any trouble obtaining a start if you live within the plant's natural growing area. If none of your friends or neighbors grow the plant, try advertising in the local paper or posting a notice at the grocery store. Or buy a commercially grown chayote fruit at the vegetable stand and plant it. Dig a shallow hole three or four inches deep, put the whole fruit in the hole and firm the soil back around the fruit, leaving the top inch of the stem end exposed. Plant at least three vines, eight to ten feet apart, to assure pollination. Provide a fence or trellis so that the vine can climb and bear its fruit off the ground.

The best soil for chayote is a fairly light, well-limed sandy loam in full sun. Insects are not usually a problem.

If you can't find a chayote fruit locally, it might be worth your while to join the True Seed Exchange. Members, who pay modest yearly dues ($2.00 a year in 1978), may trade vegetable seeds and food plant materials with other gardeners, whose offerings and needs are listed by state in an annual directory.

In cases of borderline climate or greenhouse experiment, you'll want to start your plant early indoors. Bury the whole fruit, except for the stem tip, in a pot of sandy soil in February. Keep it warm and moist until a leaf sprout appears. Then provide full sun in a warm place. Wait to set the potted vine out in the garden soil until the weather has become thoroughly warm – about the time you'd plant cantaloupes outdoors. Greenhouse-grown plants would, of course, need to be hand-pollinated in order to bear fruit. Use a soft camel's hair paintbrush to transfer the pollen from the flowers of one plant to those of another.

Corn Salad

Valerianella olitoria

Also known as lamb's-lettuce or fetticus, corn salad has been grown in European kitchen gardens since its domestication from the wild in Elizabethan times, and in America since at least the beginning of the eighteenth century, and possibly earlier. There is good reason for its continued popularity. It is a hardy, insect-resistant, mild-flavored annual green that fills in the menu in the early spring and late fall when other tender salad materials have shriveled under the influence of frost. Indeed, it will often survive the winter, if planted in a relatively sheltered spot and well mulched with some airy, non-packing material like loose straw.

Corn salad dotes on cool nights. In warm weather, it rapidly goes to seed. Once the seed stalk forms, the leaves turn bitter. Plant seed outdoors in very early spring, or at summer's end (late August or early September) for a fall crop. Plants I once started in early August promptly bolted to seed as soon as they were large enough to eat. Yet full crowns of this light-green, lobe-leafed vegetable will go on bearing well past the first frost if not subjected to heat. Thin the plants, or transplant seedlings to stand about six inches apart in rows fourteen to eighteen inches apart, or in solid beds convenient to the back door for quick picking trips in frigid weather. Corn salad is not particular as to soil, but responds well to a good humus-rich loam well supplied with lime.

The leaves are very mild – really quite bland in flavor. Most gardeners consider this a virtue, though, since there are usually enough pungent or peppery wild and tame greens around to give a salad character, but in cold weather it is often hard to find moderating greens to tone down the stronger ones in a salad. Use corn salad in tossed salads along with escarole, cress, and dandelion greens, or in a dish of mixed cooked leafy vegetables. It also combines well with the more authoritative flavor of turnip or mustard greens.

Martynia

Proboscidea jussieri

Also known as the unicorn plant, martynia was described in T. Greiner's *How to Make the Garden Pay* (1895) as 'an annual of the easiest culture – large, strong-growing, rather coarse, yet decidedly interesting.' The description still holds true. The plant reaches an average height of about two feet, with leaves as much as ten inches across and a rather viny, trailing habit. In the warm regions of the Southwest and Mexico where martynia originated, it is a perennial. Bell-shaped, catalpa-like flowers in shades of yellow, purple, and white appear in early summer, followed by three-inch-long curved, pod-like fruits with long slender curved hooks. If you'd like to follow in Grandmother's footsteps, collect a hatful of the young, tender pods and pickle them, using either your favorite sweet/sour mixture or a vinegar/brine preservative like that used for dilled cucumbers. Be sure to catch the pods while they're still young and tender if you want them for pickles.

After you've admired the flowers and eaten the pickles, let some fruits mature into the hard-shelled claw form that makes them so tempting to hobbyists. Shake out the seeds to plant next year, and use the fantastically shaped dried pods for Christmas tree ornaments, components of pod and nut wreaths, mobiles, and other decorative arrangements.

To grow the martynia or unicorn plant in most northern gardens, treat it as you would the tomato, starting seeds early indoors in pots and setting them out in the garden row after danger of frost. In relatively mild climates, you can simply sow the seed right in the garden row. Thin the plants to stand two feet apart in rows three feet wide. Seed shed from this year's plants will often volunteer new plants the following year.

Rocket
Eruca sativa

An old, old salad plant that dates back to Roman times, rocket is a fast-growing ten-inch-high leafy annual that will provide picking greens within two months of planting. Cool moist weather favors the best growth and flavor. Served either raw in salad or cooked, like spinach, rocket has – to be honest – more than a few tastier rivals, but its pungent leaves are loaded with vitamins and it is an interesting link with the gastronomy of other ages.

Scorzonera
Scorzonera hispanica

Scorzonera is also known as black salsify, but this rather ominous-sounding name is actually inaccurate. Although they resemble one another in form and even in flavor, salsify and scorzonera are unrelated. Many people who have tried both prefer scorzonera for its delicate flavor. The white-fleshed, black-skinned roots are long and thin and quite frost-hardy. Although the plant is, technically, a perennial, it is treated like an annual since it is harvested in fall and winter after spring planting. It requires about 120 days to mature. Plant the seeds in spring, as early as the ground can be worked, and thin the seedlings to stand four inches apart. Insects are seldom a problem. In fact, scorzonera is frequently planted near carrots in European gardens since it has an apparently well-deserved reputation for repelling the destructive carrot rust fly.

Try sautéing strips of scorzonera in butter, or simmering the whole scrubbed vegetable until tender and serving it with a spinach soufflé.

Skirret

Sium sisarum

A perennial root vegetable, much like a small parsnip with multiple finger-sized roots, skirret may be harvested the same season you plant it if you start with seed in early spring. The seeds share the parsnip's rather exasperating habit of germinating slowly and quite unevenly. Start the seeds indoors in flats in early spring and transplant the seedlings to a bed of well-limed, rich soil about two weeks before you expect your last frost. Space the plants ten inches apart in rows two feet apart. Skirret needs a good supply of moisture and should be watered if a week or so passes without an inch of rain.

When you harvest the roots in the fall, you'll notice that small side roots have formed. To increase your planting or share with neighbors, simply cut off these roots and replant them.

The tangle of slim roots probably accounts for skirret's fall from favor. It *does* take time to clean and prepare the roots. But the vegetable is easy to grow, fairly hardy, and not attractive to insects. Hose off the roots right in the garden and rinse them again in the kitchen after you've separated them from the crown. Because of its hard-to-clean root surface, skirret is often cooked whole until tender and *then* peeled and sliced for soups, stews, or side dishes. Sometimes the core is tough; in that case, simply slice off the tender outer meat of the vegetable in long strips and discard the core. The flavor is mild and agreeable – akin to parsnips but less sweet.

Fall Vegetable Planting

Garlic

If you want to pique your neighbors' curiosity some fine September day, tell them you're going out to do your fall vegetable planting. Even non-gardeners get seed-sowing fever in spring, and experienced gardeners make summer plantings to keep the harvest coming . . . but fall planting? Yes, it works – for certain vegetables. Think of it this way. Any vegetable that commonly volunteers (self-sows) in your garden might just as well be intentionally planted right where you want it to come up. And several cold-hardy vegetables that are most generally planted from seed in very early spring will beat all records for earliness when seed is fall-sown.

Granted, fall sowing is a bit more of a gamble than spring sowing. Not all the seeds you plant will sprout, and of the fall sprouts, not every one will live over winter. When the planting does take, however, you have an extra early crop ready to harvest in the cool spring days most conducive to its growth.

Like to gamble? Try a few of these vegetables which are usually quite reliable as fall plantings and experiment with others like turnips, kale, and chard if your winters are mild.

Spinach
Spinacia oleracea

Cool weather and short days favor the best spinach, so you can see that it's to your advantage to get a running start. Plant fresh spinach seed about one inch deep in September or October before the ground freezes. Thin the seedlings to stand six to eight inches apart. Eat the thinnings, of course! You can either plant a solid bed of spinach, as in a cold frame, or make rows twelve to fifteen inches apart. Spinach will thrive best in rich soil. When freezing weather begins, heap a loose covering of straw or hay over the young plants. Leaves may be used as a third choice, but they are a poor third since they tend to pack and mat into an impervious layer unless you've put down an armature of twigs to hold them up off the plants.

In the spring, gradually uncover the young spinach plants as the weather moderates. They will grow fast in the cool early days of March and April and you'll probably have the crop picked and eaten in time to follow it with a planting of tomatoes or beans or eggplant in May. If your winters are severe, especially if snow cover is sparse, try planting cold-resistant savoy, an especially hardy variety.

Peas

Pisum sativum

Fall planting is a bit more of a gamble with peas, but quite exhila-
rating when you get away with it. It's especially worth your while
to try this pea-planting method if your spring plantings are often
delayed by soggy wet ground which is impossible to work, especially
with tractor or Rototiller. The peas will be off and growing, taking
good advantage of the cool weather they like best before you could
ever sink a shovel in the soil.

For your first trials, choose an early variety, like Sparkle or Little
Marvel, or one of the smooth-seeded kinds like Alaska, which is
somewhat more cold-hardy than those with wrinkled seeds. Plant
the seeds an inch apart and one to two inches deep in the usual
double row with the drills spaced four to six inches apart.

You can either plant peas in late September or early October, so
that they'll germinate before killing frost, or you can wait and get
the seed in the ground just before the soil freezes hard – November
for most pea-planting regions. If the ruffled light green leaves of the
pea vines do appear above ground before killing frost, they should
be protected by an airy blanket of hay or straw when the ground is
good and cold. This will help to prevent heaving in a thaw with
consequent damage to the pea's rather shallow roots. Begin to uncover the mulch when sun regains its authority in March.

Leaf Lettuce

Lactuca sativa crispa

A small bed of leaf-lettuce, costing you little in time or money, may
be started with a mere pinch of seed. You can either broadcast the
seed in a small protected patch or cold frame or sow it right in the
garden row, which should be thoroughly dug and raked and free of
weeds. Where winters are cold but not frigid, early fall sowings of
leaf lettuce will usually live over under mulch. The most generally
useful plan, it seems to me, is to sow the seed in well-prepared
ground in November just before the soil freezes hard. Cover the bed
or row with a light layer of loose hay or straw when the ground is
frozen and gradually remove the protective cover in spring. You
might also want to try broadcasting seed right on top of bare ground
during a January or February thaw. Any one of these ploys will give

you early May lettuce – a real delicacy after a winter of what begins, in spring, to taste like secondhand vegetables.

Corn Salad
Valerianella olitoria

This age-old garden vegetable – also known as lamb's-lettuce or fetticus – may be started in fall and wintered over under mulch to yield welcome green leafy pickings during winter thaws and early spring days. Scratch the seeds into a well-raked bed of fine soil and sprinkle them if weather is dry. Thin to stand six inches apart and mulch when weather turns unremittingly cold. Not a deep colored or full flavored green, but one that is appreciated when it is most needed.

Dill
Anethum graveolens

This aromatic herb volunteers readily from self-sown seed, but if you've given your vegetable garden a thorough fall harrowing, you may want to be sure of having extra early spring dill. If so, scatter some seeds in a short row at the edge of the garden, or in an herb bed, in October or November (planted much earlier, the seeds would sprout but the seedlings might not live over). Rake one-quarter to one-half inch of loose fine soil over the seeds and make a note on the calendar to watch for the first early dill snippets next March or April.

Parsley
Petroselinum hortense

Notorious for its slow germination, which can take as long as a month in the cold spring soil, parsley is worth a try as a fall-sown crop. It was, after all, an old custom to leave a seed head dangling from the garden gate or a nearby tree to ensure a yearly crop of parsley. Use fresh seed, sow it in fine, well-raked, and weeded soil in October or November, and mark the spot. If seedlings do germinate in the fall, cover them with a fluffy layer of straw mulch. Far from a sure thing, fall parsley planting is nevertheless a worthwhile gamble – one that just might pay off in early parsley next spring, without all that fingernail chewing.

Garlic
Allium sativum

If you've ever grown garlic and found strong new flat-leaved spears with that unmistakable aroma in the garden when planting your peas the following spring, you won't need to be convinced of garlic's hardiness. The secret is to plant the individual cloves, blunt end down, four inches apart and two to three inches deep in early or mid fall. In mild winter climates the top greenery will continue to grow all winter and produce extra large bulbs the following summer. Even if you get what sometimes seems like more than your share of cold and snow, this trick is worth trying. Garlic escapees lived over in my garden through a winter of record cold, and intentional plantings made in well-prepared rich weed-free soil do even better. The bulbs will be ready for harvest in July or August but may be used up to a month earlier when they will be very juicy, but difficult to peel.

Growing Perennial Vegetables from Seed

Watercress

Gardeners are always planning ahead. '*Next* year I'll plant this, do that, dig up more garden, try this new technique.' If you can look beyond next season in your garden, you'd be wise to plant some perennial vegetables. They will give you good eating for many years to come. Furthermore, if you start the plants from seed, you will have, at a cost of a dollar or less, a whole plantation of perennials, assuring you of plenty for both eating fresh and freezing, year after year.

Seed-grown perennials do not take too much longer to achieve bearing age than those you purchase as rooted plants. Mail-order plants are often held back considerably by loss of fine feeder roots and the period of time they spend in cold storage. Plants you raise from seed may be kept growing steadily from the seedling stage and may be further selected for vigor and good root development when you transplant them to the permanent bed. In many cases, they will catch up to – and often surpass – older transplants.

Planting perennial vegetables involves a certain commitment. Since they will occupy the same garden space for years, any soil improvements you make before planting will be effort well spent. It is also important to make your perennial plantings either in a separate bed or in a row at the edge of the garden where they may be left undisturbed if you till or plow the garden plot.

Asparagus
Asparagus officinalis

If you have room for only one perennial vegetable, make it asparagus. A bed of asparagus is a lifetime investment, so choose the spot with care. Asparagus likes rich soil, well limed and well drained. There is a persistent rumor that it requires applications of salt, but this is really just an inverted – and inaccurate – version of the fact that asparagus is historically a seaside plant and it tolerates salt spray. Don't salt your asparagus!

You would do well to begin preparing the asparagus bed about the time you are ready to sow the seed in flats or in a nursery row. (You could also plant the seeds directly in the permanent bed, but transplanting them gives you greater control over spacing and seedling quality). Mix limestone and bone meal with compost or well-rotted manure and dig it into the plot where you intend to plant your asparagus bed. Let the mixture mellow while you start the seeds.

For indoor planting, sow asparagus seed in three-inch-deep flats in

February or early March. Keep them under fluorescent lights or at a sunny window until early April, when you can start to harden them off. This gradual adjustment to the stresses of outdoor life – wind, hot sun, ultraviolet light, pelting rain – should begin with the plants basking in a partly shady, sheltered spot for several hours on a mild day, progressing, over a period of at least a week, to complete exposure to the sun, at which time the seedlings may be transplanted to their permanent position, or set five inches apart, in a nursery row for another year.

You might, on the other hand, want to follow the easier course of planting seed in a nursery row around apple-blossom time, thinning to a five- to six-inch spacing, and transplanting the seedlings to their reserved row in summer, fall, or the following spring.

Time of transplanting seems to matter less than care of the roots at this critical time. Ideally, only a few plants at a time should be dug and the roots replanted promptly. If you have many transplants to deal with, cover them with a wet burlap bag if the roots have soil around them, or soak them in a bucket of water if the roots are bare.

Asparagus seedlings are delightfully promising, with the feathery tops and strong roots of the species. They will grow at least a foot tall, and often more, in their first year. Don't ever allow anyone to mow down the ferny greenery, in either seedling or mature plants, for it is the tops that create the nourishment to sustain the roots.

There was a time when the planting of an asparagus bed called for heroic measures like digging trenches three feet deep. That's an effective – if strenuous – way to plant asparagus and there's nothing wrong with it. All that effort is not really necessary, though. Gardeners who have examined the evidence have concluded that asparagus may be planted much more shallowly. In fact, plantings made just under the soil surface – four to five inches deep – do very well. Deeper planted roots will erupt somewhat later in the spring. Thus you can stagger your harvest by digging roots in at different levels . . . a foot, eight, six, and four inches deep.

What deep digging *did* do for asparagus was to loosen the soil under the crown, and that probably accounted for much of the success of the method, for asparagus really puts forth when it has good drainage and well-aerated soil. If you want to give your plants a super start, you can achieve the same effect by digging a trench one foot deep and running your Rototiller along the bottom of the trench to loosen the soil. Then space mounds of loose soil mixed with compost at intervals of fifteen to eighteen inches in the trench. Drape the roots over the sides of the mounds and pat more loose soil to cover them. Even young seedlings will have a surprisingly extensive network of white string-like roots.

Your asparagus patch should receive a yearly application of fertilizer. My own preference is for well-rotted manure. Mulch will help, too, to control weeds and retain moisture – and to gradually feed those prodigious roots, which may range as far as five to six feet in each direction. Make parallel rows of asparagus four feet apart. The bed or row should be no less than three feet from any other garden perennial. The asparagus beetle, which can denude the top growth and weaken the plant, can be deterred by hand-picking and by planting tomatoes nearby.

Picking – the moment we're all waiting for – begins in the third year (two years after planting), *if* there are finger-thick spears. Harvest for no more than two weeks and then let the plants develop their ferny tops. In the fourth year, you can pick for a month or six weeks, as long as spears remain large enough, but no spears under pencil size should be taken. After the fourth year, picking may continue for as long as eight to ten weeks, as long as the spears maintain their size.

Our asparagus bed has reached this marvelous condition of maturity and we find it possible, each spring, to eat asparagus almost daily for the better part of two months – either steamed for dinner, served with toast for lunch, or cut raw into a salad. We never tire of it. Can you *imagine* ever having too much asparagus?

Globe Artichokes
Cynara scolymus

Unlike the hardy, enduring asparagus, globe artichokes are much more exotic, tender, and capricious. You certainly can't count on them, as you can asparagus, for carefree permanent harvests. They are, in fact, commercially grown only in a limited area in California where winters are mild and air is very damp and foggy. I would not have even considered planting them in my garden, until, after mentioning globe artichokes in one of my gardening columns in *Country Journal* magazine, I received a letter, complete with color photo, from some readers – Vermont residents, at that – who had successfully raised two of the large thistle-like plants and harvested seven globes the first season. After that, I heard about two more gardeners, also in New England, who had harvested this delicacy from homegrown plants. One had even raised his artichoke plants from seed. (The others had started with mail-order plants.)

What was their secret? They were, for one thing, determined to succeed, and so in each case the plants were coaxed along and given the best of care and protection. Ultra-rich soil, plenty of lime, a sunny, sheltered spot, and abundant moisture (but good drainage) provided the sort of conditions on which globe artichokes are known to thrive. Eliot Coleman, director of the Small Farm Research Association and the man who had grown his plants from seed, put his finger on one growing technique that might have made a difference. As perennials, globe artichokes would not normally have flowered until their second year. (The fleshy-petalled bud of the flower, of course, is the edible delicacy for which we pay high prices at food stores, when and if they are available.) Coleman theorizes, though, that an early chilling his plants endured when they were still in the seedling stage could have forced them to set buds. The same thing had happened earlier to a flat of celery seedlings he had inadvertently chilled, although in the case of celery the planting was a loss because it is celery's vegetative stage, not its flowers or seeds, that appeals to gardeners and eaters. This process, known as vernalization, has actually been used experimentally to make peppers and tomatoes form early blooms and fruit.

Plant globe artichoke seeds indoors in February or March, in individual pots, and keep the seedlings on a sunny windowsill or under fluorescent lights. Wait to plant them out until the weather has settled and there is no more danger of frost – at least a week after you put out your tomatoes.

The best way to ensure that the plant enjoys the necessary combined conditions of rich soil, abundant moisture, and good drainage is to incorporate plenty of humus in the soil. If you have only a little bit of compost, spend it here. Mix at least one good shovelful of compost, well-aged manure, or leaf mold in advanced decay, into the planting hole when setting out the young plants.

Flower buds form first at the end of the main stem and, later, at the tips of the side branches. If you're especially eager for your first taste of homegrown artichoke, indulge yourself; the buds are at their tender best when the fleshy green bracts are still smoothly closed. Picked young enough – about the size of a large lemon – the chokes may even be cut in half and eaten whole. Even a mature artichoke with its bracts partly opened like those you buy in the market will be a sumptuous treat when you've grown it yourself.

Artichokes are exquisitely susceptible to fungus disease. For that reason, it is crucially important to provide good drainage and prevent pooling of water around the crown of the plant. Also avoid setting the plant too low in the ground, or its central bud may become waterlogged and decayed. When you begin to harvest chokes (oh, lucky day!) trim the stem off right at ground level rather than leaving a protruding stump in which disease might start and spread to the rest of the plant.

Bringing a globe artichoke through the winter in cold climates is an achievement in itself – crop or no crop. At least the New England-grown plants were spared the hazard of alternate thawing and freezing that, in more moderate climates, often kills plants by tearing their roots.

To winter over a globe artichoke plant successfully, you must protect it from both temperature extremes and waterlogging. Many northern gardeners cut the plant back to a height of fifteen inches or so in order to minimize the possibility of having a large frozen leaf mass decaying over the central crown. At any rate, in any area where winter freezes are expected, the artichoke bush should have a generous armful of straw heaped over its crown and covered with a bushel basket to prevent compacting. Then, as a final touch, heap aged manure around and over the basket. Be careful when uncovering plants in the spring. It is easy to inadvertently knock off the tender new sprouts.

Globe artichoke plants generally produce for three to five years. When they are well established, they send out new offset shoots, which may be dug and replanted to renew the bed. Growing these sought-after exotics takes plenty of patience, skill, a free hand with the compost, and more than a little luck. Seed-grown plants tend to vary widely in their characteristics, though, so if your first planting should disappoint you, try again. If they can do it in New England, you can probably do it too, unless you live in one of the colder parts of Canada.

Sorrel

Rumex acetosa

Sorrel is an obliging perennial that you can raise with your left hand while your right hand is otherwise occupied. Unflinchingly hardy, easy to raise from seed, quick to produce, and exceptionally rich in vitamins A and C, sorrel not only lives over, but may often actually be plucked from beneath January snow, if it occupies a sheltered spot. You can plant it anywhere, even in part shade. With its deep, strong, energy-storing root, it needs no special winter protection. I started seeds indoors in flats in March and set them outside late in April, but you could just as easily sow them right in the garden row, thinning the seedlings to stand six to eight inches apart in rows spaced about fifteen inches apart. The long, thin, piquantly acid-flavored leaves are at their best in cool weather. Mix them with other steamed greens, cook them in soup or chop a few young tender leaves in the evening salad (and use one to two tablespoons less vinegar than usual).

Watercress
Nasturtium officinale

Watercress is a real specialist. It is at its best in a flowing, well-aerated stream, preferably in limestone soil. Unfortunately, not every gardener has that kind of facility in the backyard. The streams on our property are small and barely there during the summer and the soil is acid-leaning ironstone, a far cry from limestone. Nevertheless, I've had the pleasure of serving my family large bouquets of fresh green watercress from a bed I've established at the edge of our pond where an underground spring enters the water. Plants I'd begged from friends never took, but young seedlings I started indoors under lights in late February, and dug into the pond bank in April, multiplied into a four-by-four-foot bed by fall – a delightfully dependable source of soup and salad greenery that doesn't require maintenance. The cress chokes out weeds and it is quite well watered.

Plant the fine seeds in a clay pot, as thinly as you can, for germination is quite complete. Keep the pot in a shallow pan of water. Transplant the seedlings to other clay pots filled with good potting soil and space them about two inches apart in the pot. Stand the containers in pans of water and keep them constantly supplied with water until time to set them out.

Even without a stream or pond, you can grow a small but steady supply of watercress by keeping the potted seedlings, always with their feet in water, in a partly sunny spot and fertilizing them weekly. Since cress seems to prefer well-aerated water, changing the water in the pan daily will help to keep them happy. I grew watercress on my porch in this way last summer, just to see whether it could be done. The plants produced less than those by the pond, but it was real watercress and it was good.

Sweet Potatoes Forever

Sweet Potato

Sweet Potatoes

Ipomoea batatas

Learning to grow sweet potatoes is a new venture for many gardeners. Although sweets require no more care than tomatoes or lettuce, they are often overlooked when the garden plan is made out. I don't know why this should be so, for sweets are delicious, easy to grow, and widely enjoyed. If you want to find out what you've been missing, you can start by planting a summer crop of these heat-loving but trouble-free delicacies, progress to the point where you can store the sweets so that they will keep all winter, and achieve advanced standing by managing to start new plants in spring from sound roots you've kept over from the fall harvest.

Consider, first, what sweet potatoes require. An essentially undemanding plant, the sweet (*Ipomoea batatas*) is a member of the morning glory family. Its one absolute requirement is for a good 150 days of frost-free weather. A native of the tropics, the vine grows best at a temperature range of 70 to 85 degrees F. At 60 degrees F. it stops growing, and prolonged temperatures below 50 degrees F. retard the plant. While sweet potatoes are not raised commercially much above the latitude of New Jersey, they are successfully grown in home gardens as far north as Michigan, Wisconsin, Connecticut, and even Massachusetts. In cold borderline climates, the plants will perform better if they are grown in sandy soil, which warms quickly. Some gardeners use black plastic mulch to boost heat retention in the soil. A raised bed or row-long ridge of loose soil will also be warmer than the surrounding ground. Or, if you're short of space, you might try planting the vines in a long, narrow (six to eight inches wide) foot-deep box on a sunny patio or porch, or even on your roof.

Contrary to popular opinion, you can grow sweet potatoes in clay soil, as long as your garden isn't afflicted with severe hardpan – a layer of impervious, compacted soil under the garden. Although sweets are traditionally grown in acid soil (pH 5.2 to 6.7), the reason for this practice is disease control, not the intrinsic requirements of the plant. Some diseases, especially in warmer Southern climates, are more troublesome in neutral or alkaline soil.

On the whole, though, sweet potatoes don't need much special care. They produce well even in dry weather and poor soil. An excess of nitrogen will make them mature late, especially in a rainy season. Go lightly on the manure when preparing the bed. Tubers harvested from plants grown in high-nitrogen soil tend to be long and thin rather than chunky. A deficiency of potassium in the soil will also promote spindly roots. Wood ashes, greensand, granite dust, or spoiled hay, dug in at spring planting or fall clean-up time, will help to supply needed potassium (also called potash). Insect problems are not common.

For your first sweet potato row, you'll probably have to buy rooted slips, either from a mail-order supplier or from a farmers' market, if you're lucky enough to live near one. (See list of sources.) One hundred plants will be ample for a family of four to eat fresh and store for winter use. Since sweet potato plants are held back by cold weather, your best planting time is two weeks after your last spring frost. Here in south central Pennsylvania, for example, our last spring frost occurs about May 14 and I plant sweet potatoes over Memorial Day weekend.

The slips you receive in the mail will look most unpromising, to put it kindly. Don't worry, though. They're more alive than they look. Put the roots in water, if possible, for a day before planting. You'll need a little time to prepare the row. The vines will ramble, so allow four feet between rows. Rototill or dig and rake the soil to a fine tilth. Then go down your row on each side, using a rake or hoe to draw soil from the row middles to form a ridge along the planting line.

Now, to plant the slips, start with the largest, strongest ones in case you run out of room. I use a long-bladed trowel to settle the rooted slips in the soft ridged-up soil about twelve to fourteen inches apart. If your soil is good and loose, you can use the short-forked end of a stick to push the roots down into the ridge. At the end of each fifteen-foot row – or, better yet, as each plant is settled into the earth – the slips should be well watered into the soil to help settle the roots. I always toss a light sprinkling of hay or straw over the plants, too, to protect them from the bright summer sun. By the time the vines grow high enough to peek over their light protective covering, their roots are well established and no more watering for hoeing is needed, even in a very dry season.

Before the vines start to spread, though, I mulch the four feet of bare soil between the rows with old hay or coarse cut weeds, more for weed control than for moisture retention.

From then on, the sweet potatoes are on their own until harvest time. In the warm southerly climate which is their native home, sweet potato plants are allowed to remain in the ground until the leaves turn yellow, indicating that the plant is mature. Most North

American gardeners, though, must harvest the sweets as soon as frost hits the vines. We enjoy snitching some tubers early in September to confirm the approach of fall, but we try to hold off on the main harvest as long as possible, for the tubers will double in size every week throughout the month of September. They'll continue to grow in October, of course, providing frost is late, but at a somewhat slower rate.

Tubers should be dug immediately after frost has darkened and wilted the leaves, for continued cold nights will damage them if they're left in the ground. Using a spading fork, dig from the side of the row to avoid slicing potatoes or nicking them. Bruised potatoes rot readily, and it doesn't take much violence to bruise a sweet, so lay them gently in the wheelbarrow rather than tossing them on from a distance. Brush the loose dirt from the sweets and spread them out in the sun to dry for the rest of the day. Take a few moments to gloat over the largest specimens you've unearthed. There's nothing uniform about homegrown sweet potatoes; some will be huge, some medium, some small. The tiny fingerling potatoes are tender and delicious cooked whole, in the skin.

Actually, the skin of a newly dug sweet potato is very thin, almost wispy when cooked. Because there is such a thin barrier between the sweet potato and the outside world, sweets spoil readily unless well cured. The curing process toughens the skin and reduces the internal water content of the potato. To cure your sweet potatoes, spread them in a single layer in a hot place – 80 to 90 degrees F. – for two weeks. We keep ours behind the wood stove in our kitchen and by the time we learn to avoid stumbling over them, the two weeks have passed and it's time to pack them away for the winter.

For winter storage, keep the potatoes in a dry, well-ventilated place between 50 and 60 degrees F. As you've probably discovered if you've ever tried to store sweets in the refrigerator, cold, damp places encourage sweet potatoes to rot. I wrap each sweet individually in a piece of newspaper and pile them loosely in a basket, which spends the winter in a cool upstairs room. Some shrivel or mummify, usually the very small ones, but enough of them make it through till spring to go with the Easter ham.

If you harvest your sweet potatoes carefully, cure them well, and store them dry at 50 to 60 degrees F., you should have no trouble keeping a good supply over the winter. Having accomplished this feat, you're now ready to start *this* year's sweet potato plants from *last* year's tubers. This part is fun and a fine antidote to the late winter doldrums.

Begin about two months before planting-out time – even earlier, if you wish – to root slips from several of your best potatoes: chunky, sound ones that have kept well. A medium-sized sweet potato has about fifty eyes, each of which will sprout into a new plant. The secret to persuading them to sprout is *constant warmth*. Suspend the sweet potato in a jar of water and keep it warm until you see sprouts forming. I keep my sprouting sweets on the pilot light of my gas stove. Having read about studies indicating that a solution of seaweed extract promotes sprouting in sweet potatoes, I now add kelp at the recommended concentration – one tablespoon of kelp to one quart of water – to the water in which I sprout my potatoes.

Some gardeners bury the sweets in damp sand or Vermiculite and keep them in a warm spot. The farmers' wives who sell sweet potato slips at our local farmers' market usually start them in a hot bed, made by piling eight inches of manure in a cold frame, covering it with two inches of soil and pressing the potatoes into this bedding. They are watered regularly and kept warm. When the sun is intense, the top sash of the cold frame should be raised for ventilation.

You can twist off the slips and plant them directly in the ground, but I prefer to remove them from the potato before the roots tangle and set them three inches apart in good potting soil in a four-inch-deep container (an old refrigerator crisper or dishpan works well). They spend a few weeks growing roots and leafy green tops in a protected setting, under fluorescent lights or in the cold frame, before being planted out.

And so the year has come full circle, but this time the plants are your own. You'll probably find, as I have, that the homegrown slips will take hold and grow at least two weeks ahead of purchased plants and have a much lower mortality rate. Your other advantages will be intangible, but nonetheless real – the satisfaction of having learned a new technique and the feeling of self-sufficiency that comes with knowing that you can provide for yourself.

Oriental Vegetables

Burdock

At least 300,000 species of plants have been identified, but there are still thousands of other species of plants growing on earth that have not yet been described and named. Sometimes I ponder this awesome fact when I'm trying to decide whether to serve carrots or beans for dinner. Not all of these undiscovered treasures are food plants, of course. Still, there are many, many more species of food-producing plants in the world than most people realize. Vegetables are supremely important in the Orient especially, where not enough arable land is available to raise grain for feeding livestock. Their flavor and texture *make* the meal. Since vegetables are so necessary and so widely appreciated in China and Japan, many different kinds are grown – some of which are just beginning to be introduced here in America. Not so incidentally, the marvelous cuisine that has developed around fresh vegetables in these ancient cultures is now recognized as an eminently sane way to eat, and more productive of health than overnutrition based on heavy use of red meat, saturated fat, and sugar.

For something interesting and delicious to serve along with your familiar garden standbys, or for a truly authentic Chinese or Japanese meal, you might like to try growing and cooking some of these special Oriental vegetables. There are many, a few of them suitable only for warm climates. I'll describe here a representative group of leaf, root, and fruiting vegetables that seem to me, from my experiments with them, to be good choices. This is the first, rather than the last word on Oriental vegetables, then, but I hope it will introduce you to a delightful world of growing things that will give you pleasure and do you good.

Burdock
Arctium lappa

Great gobo, as burdock is sometimes called, is a robust plant. Its strong roots often grow to a depth of three feet and the sturdy stems bearing large leaves usually reach a height of three to four feet; even six feet is not uncommon. Closely related to the common weedy burdock of the wayside, *Arctium minus*, garden burdock is cultivated for its somewhat milder flavor. Children often call the burdock plant 'wild rhubarb' or 'elephant ears.' Its large, ovoid, wavy-edged leaves are borne on stalks resembling those of an old, tough rhubarb plant.

Burdock is most commonly grown (or gathered from the wild) for its root, which, when peeled, has an agreeable crispness and pungency. Spring-planted burdock roots are at their best in late summer. Later, when the plant blooms, the root will be tough and woody. In the Orient, young burdock shoots are often cooked and eaten like asparagus.

Plant the seeds in mid spring in rows at least eighteen inches apart. Thin the seedlings to stand six inches apart. Gardeners who are really serious about getting good long roots often dig the soil deeply before planting. Burdock is pretty much insect- and disease-free. Don't let the plant go to seed in the garden, though, or even the cultivated variety will become a nuisance.

The root must be dug, for it is too long and slender to pull up. Naturalist Euell Gibbons discovered a good way to harvest large quantities of burdock. As he relates in his book *Stalking the Wild Asparagus*, he would dig a hole next to the plant with a post-hole digger and then pull the adjacent roots over into the hole. After a rain, when the ground is soft, it is not difficult to dig up foot-long pieces of the root with an ordinary shovel.

The one-inch-thick root must be peeled before cooking, or it will be disagreeably bitter. It is often stir-fried or cooked in soup stock. For milder flavor, some cooks parboil the root slices, discard the cooking water and boil again for twenty to thirty minutes. Pre-soaking reduces some of the pungent flavor too, but at the expense of some of the water-soluble vitamins. I served much of our last year's burdock crop according to a suggestion in *Johnny's Selected Seed Catalogue*: cut the peeled root into chunks and poke the pieces into a pot of baked beans just before you put the beans into the oven to bake.

Cee Gwa

Luffa acutangula

Some seed catalogues refer to Cee gwa as 'Chinese okra.' There is a resemblance between the slim, ridged, six-inch-long fruits of this member of the cucurbit family and the pods of an okra plant, but they are not related botanically. Actually an edible gourd, Cee gwa thrives in warm weather and rich soil. Fruits appear about three months after planting. Northern gardeners can get a head start on a crop of Cee gwa by sowing seeds in peat pots in the house and planting them outside after danger of frost is past.

This is a good plant to train to a trellis or fence by tying up the vines as they grow. The plants should be spaced about six inches apart in the row. If you are starting with seed, of course, you would sow the seeds about two inches apart and thin to retain the strongest plants at the wider spacing.

Pick the fruits when they're young and tender. The older gourds turn tough and fibrous. Young Cee gwa may be used like zucchini or cucumbers: with their ridges trimmed off, they may be served raw in salads or cooked (steam or stir-fry) in soups or side dishes.

Chinese Cabbage

Bok Choy (leafy), *Brassica chinensis*

Wong Bok (heading), *Brassica pekinensis*

It is natural, I suppose, to explain an unfamiliar vegetable in terms of a more familiar one. Still, the term 'cabbage' never seems to me to properly describe this vegetable, which, in its two forms, is quite a different food from the widely grown solid round heads we use to make cole slaw. Like the related round-headed garden cabbage, Wong bok and Bok choy are good steamed and buttered, or cooked in soup. It is in salads that they excell, though, particularly in late fall when lettuce has given out. The leaves are more tender than those of common garden cabbage, and the base and heart have the crispness of celery without the strings, and with a mild flavor.

Most varieties of Wong bok and Bok choy go to seed quickly if they mature in hot weather. Consequently, unless you plant one of the recently introduced heat resistant strains like Spring A-1, you'll have a larger, tastier harvest if you plant the seed in summer for a fall crop. June and July plantings do well for me. We eat the thinnings in August and September and cut the mature plant in October, or even November if I've given them some protection from frost.

Sow the seeds in rows eighteen to twenty-four inches apart or in a solid bed, and thin seedlings to stand eighteen to twenty-four inches apart in the row. Good fertile soil and a steady supply of moisture help to produce tender, fast-growing leaves. Unlike regular cabbage, Wong bok and Bok choy often die when transplanted, so the seeds must be sown where they are to grow.

Daikon

Raphanus sativus longipinnatus (Oriental radishes)

As ubiquitous in Japan as the potato is in America, these large Oriental radishes are more substantial and versatile than our small crisp early spring radishes. They are served raw, either sliced or grated, steamed as a vegetable, cooked in soup, and pickled. Plant the seed in early spring, in rows twelve to fifteen inches apart as you would radishes or turnips. Thin the seedlings of large Daikon varieties so that they are spaced ten inches apart in the row. Early summer plantings will yield a fall crop that may be stored in a cold place for a month or two. You can't do that with a delicate spring radish.

Good varieties to try include:

MIYASHIGE, fine quality thick, blunt root. A good fall crop which is good for storage. Plant in midsummer.

SAKURAJIMA, famous for its ability to achieve prodigious size.

TOKINASHE, sow in spring or summer. The pointed roots are pungent.

For an introduction to Daikon relish, try mixing equal parts of the grated raw root with cooked, coarsely grated beets and seasoning the mixture with salt and lemon juice.

Gai Choy

Brassica juncea (Chinese mustard greens)

A planting of Gai choy makes good use of garden space. These leafy greens are ready to pluck about five weeks after planting. We like them because they have a rich but mild flavor; they're not at all pungent or bitter like some greens. Be sure to pick them young, though, for they shoot to flower as soon as the weather turns hot. We use the whole plant top, snipping leaves and stems into a pan of butter for brief sautéing.

Plant Gai choy in early spring and thin the seedlings to a three- to four-inch spacing. (Save the thinnings for the evening's soup.) Flea beetles, tiny black jumping insects that chew small round holes in the leaves, can be hard on seedlings of Gai choy and other members of the cabbage family. Powdered diatomaceous earth, available as Perma Guard from some seedsmen, helps to control flea beetles without poisoning the vegetable or the soil.

Gai Lohn

Brassica alboglabra (Chinese broccoli)

Although the florets are smaller and less solid than those of the more familiar Western broccoli, both leaves and stem are good to eat. Pick the flower buds before they bloom in order to enjoy them at their best. Gai lohn is often stir-fried and served while still tender-crisp and bright green. When steaming the vegetable, cook it briefly, stopping short of that unappetizing gray-green shade too often seen in overcooked broccoli.

Gai lohn thrives in rich soil and cool weather. Its best growth periods are in spring and fall, so it is a good vegetable to plant in early spring and again in midsummer for fall use. Space the plants about six inches apart in rows at least one foot apart.

Gow Choy

Allium odoratum (Chinese chives)

Easy to grow, decorative and versatile, this perennial member of the onion family forms handsome clumps of slender flat leaves. The flavor has more than a hint of garlic and blends pleasingly with many salads and mixed meat and vegetable dishes. I like to add the finely snipped leaves shortly before serving time; long cooking makes them limp and stringy.

You can sow seeds of Gow choy right in the garden row or do as I did: start little plants in the house in late winter and plant them out in the garden in April. Light frost won't hurt the seedlings and when the plants are well established, by season's end, they'll be strong enough to endure winter freezes if covered with a protective mulch. Space the plants eight to ten inches apart in rows at least a foot apart or plant them in an herb bed in groups. You can start cutting the tops when they're five or six inches high and continue to cut throughout the season as new growth appears.

Heung Kuhn

Apium graveolens (Chinese celery)

This is a slow-growing plant, somewhat less robust than Western celery. When planted in April, Heung kuhn forms an eight-inch-wide clump of thin leafy celery stalks by August. It is useful as a flavoring plant. I add a leaf or two, and a few chopped stems, to soups, stews, and casseroles. Sometimes I dry the leaves, too, to use in the same way over winter. Sow seeds of Heung kuhn in March in peat pots or seed flats in the house. Plant it out in late April or early May, spacing the plants eight to ten inches apart. Rich soil and a steady supply of moisture will assure a succulent stem and a bushy crop of leaves. Insects don't seem to bother the plants, which are quite cold-hardy but should be protected from hard frosts.

Hinn Choy

Amaranthus gangeticus (Chinese spinach)

Hinn choy is a good warm-weather spinach. Plants set out in April or May will be just right for eating by midsummer, when the early cool-weather greens have petered out. Plant seeds in rows twelve to fifteen inches apart and thin seedlings to stand four inches apart. Once Hinn choy plants are several inches high they tend to suffer a severe setback when transplanted. I've gotten away with transplanting very young seedlings, though. I started the seeds in flats kept on an east porch and transplanted the seedlings to the garden row when they were about an inch high, taking care to retain a small ball of soil around the roots, to water them in well, and to shade them for two days.

Hinn choy likes warm weather. Since it is ready in about forty-five days after planting it may be seeded in the row after an early planting of radishes and still have a chance to grow to harvest size, with time to spare, before fall frost. Amaranth plants vary more widely than many garden vegetables; most are green but you may find some with mahogany red leaves or streaks. The flavor is mild and good, blending well with other sharper-flavored greens in a mixture.

Mao Gwa

Benincasa hispida (Fuzzy gourd)

Now that the pet rock craze has run its course, why not a pet vegetable? This fuzzy gourd is a good candidate. The four- to five-inch-long fruits assume a comfortable rounded pear shape when fully developed. The green rind is somewhat tougher than that of a zucchini, and the fuzz must be peeled off before cooking. The plant is a tender, rambling vine that grows somewhat like a cucumber vine. It will perform best when given some support – tied to a trellis, fence, or wooden rack. Plant seeds after danger of frost, when soil is warm. (I like to pre-sprout them in damp paper towels and tuck the sprouted seed gently under one inch of compost in the row.) Rows should be three feet apart with plants spaced about every six inches. Mao gwa likes comfort and luxury – warm weather, rich soil, and a steady supply of moisture (one inch per week). The sliced cooked fruits look and taste like a slightly meatier zucchini. We like them in mixed vegetable soup, and braised with onions.

Shungiku
Chrysanthemum coronarium

Some of the Oriental vegetables mentioned above have Western counterparts, but Shungiku is in a class by itself. Although the term 'Chop suey greens' has also been applied to Shungiku, it is actually an edible variety of chrysanthemum. The leaves of this hardy annual have the familiar chrysanthemum-like lobes, and the yellow, single-petaled, daisy-like flower forms a bright note amid the gray-green cauliflower and brussels sprouts of late summer.

Despite some seed catalog warnings about its pungency, we found Shungiku to be a pleasantly aromatic addition to a salad or a pan of stir-fried vegetables. It is not the sort of vegetable you'd prepare by the bucketful. The pungency is not at all on the sharp or bitter side, though, more on the order of garden mint, a plant you wouldn't eat by the cupful either, but one which also makes a splendid subtle flavor contribution when used in small amounts.

If you like to try new flavors, do sample some Shungiku. Plant seed in early spring in rows ten to fifteen inches apart, or even in solid beds in an herb garden. When the leaves have grown to a height of six inches, you can start to harvest them, either by pulling the whole plant to thin the row (three to four inch spacing is about right) or cutting the leaves and letting more grow. Flavor is best before the plant blooms but I've snipped a few leaves from a blooming plant into our lunch-time salad and no one complained.

Raising Vegetables in the Closet

Lettuce

Those for whom the gardening season begins outdoors in March or April are sometimes surprised to hear how many vegetables can be grown indoors, under lights. You can raise the ingredients of a luscious bowl of tossed salad under a pair of fluorescent light tubes any time . . . even in the depths of winter when the garden outside is frozen ringing hard or drifted deep in snow. If you're looking for an off-season gardening project that will put some fresh food on the table, you might like to try adventuring in this direction.

Your first step will be to arrange your light set-up. Forget all the confusing and intimidating things you've heard about the many available kinds of fluorescent light tubes. If you want to use the special full-spectrum Plant Growth tubes, go right ahead, but you really don't need them if you're growing non-flowering plants. You can use ordinary household fluorescents. It *is* a good idea, when possible, to pair a warm white tube with a cool white one; both are usually available at hardware stores.

Fluorescent tubes consume considerably less power than incandescents for the amount of illumination they provide. They are sized by wattage, a 40-watt tube being longer than a 20-watt tube, but no brighter. The longer tubes are more efficient, however, since light intensity falls off at the extreme ends of the tubes. For this reason, I'd recommend using 40-watt bulbs if at all possible. Although they may appear large in the beginning, you will find that there are all sorts of plants you want to put under them, and before long the space under the lights will be crowded with greenery. The short 20-watt light fixture I started with helped me to discover what I could grow under lights. I've since become so addicted to year-round gardening, though, that I now use a large four-shelf cart with two pairs of 40-watt (48 inches long) fluorescent tubes on each tier. (Someday I hope to have a solar greenhouse in operation, but until I do, I use my lights gratefully and cut down on power usage in other ways . . . by continuing not to miss the dryer, dishwasher, or TV I never really wanted anyway!)

Where will you put your lights? Wherever they'll fit! You can use a dark, unused corner like a closet, pantry, basement shelf, or even coalbin, or perhaps a spare bedroom, a wall in the bathroom, or a section of kitchen counter under the cabinets. The spot you choose should have reasonably good air circulation and a temperature above 50 degrees F. You can suspend a two-tube fixture by chains or even macrame rope, or you might want to attach it to the underside of a shelf or cabinet. Use at least two tubes in your installation. A single tube does not shed enough light to foster the growth of indoor vegetables. Two pairs of tubes mounted in a parallel arrangement are even more efficient than one pair, but are not really necessary unless you're growing tomatoes indoors.

Plant your vegetable seeds in flats or clay pots filled with a mixture of equal parts of potting soil, vermiculite, and leaf mold or compost, or in any other growing medium you may prefer. Avoid using plain garden soil unmixed with lightening modifiers like vermiculite or perlite, because the soil will become hard and densely packed when used indoors, leaving no room for plant roots to grow. It is especially important to plant seeds thinly for these indoor vegetable gardens. Crowded seedlings will not mature into first-rate plants. Allow an inch between seeds.

The containers of germinating seeds should be kept relatively warm; 70 to 75 degrees F. is a good range. The seedlings and growing plants of most of the reliable light-nurtured vegetables will do well at considerably lower temperatures – 50 to 65 degrees F. Keep seedling flats warm and damp until sprouts appear and put them under lights, very close to (but not touching) the tubes as soon as you see signs of life. All of the vegetables I've grown indoors have done well with sixteen to eighteen hours of light each day. Plants should receive no more than eighteen hours of light in a twenty-four-hour period, though; they need those hours of darkness to convert the starches and sugars they've formed under the influence of light into new tissue.

The vegetables that have produced best for me under lights are all cool-weather plants.

Lettuce
Lactuca sativa

Lettuce is a good choice for your first indoor food growing experiments. Bibb and Boston have been my favorite varieties. Boston lettuce grows fast and remains tender. Bibb, although somewhat slower to achieve the same size, forms loose heads of crisper, darker green leaves. I sow seeds in a small flat and transplant the seedlings to six-inch deep containers when they have their first true leaves. Refrigerator crisper drawers and square plastic wash basins make good indoor lettuce beds. Space the plants four to five inches apart. From seed to salad plant takes fifty-two days for me. Sowing small amounts of seed every three to four weeks will ensure a continuous supply.

Lettuce is shallow-rooted and needs plenty of moisture. I feed my plants once a week with diluted fish-emulsion fertilizer. Pale yellow leaves indicate a hungry plant. Feed it in installments a day or two apart, though, rather than overcompensating with a large fertilizer feeding, and never apply fertilizer at a higher concentration than recommended on the label.

Radishes
Raphanus sativus

Radishes grown under lights take about six weeks to develop. They are, surprisingly, often milder flavored than those grown outdoors. Thin the seedlings to stand about one and one-half inches apart and keep them cool and well watered. Don't bother to replant thinnings; they don't transplant well. You can grow a bunch of radishes in a five-inch pot. Keep several going at different stages. If you use a flat, it should be at least three inches deep, preferably four inches. There's something about pulling a radish out of a flowerpot in January that makes the wind howling outside a bit less formidable.

Carrots
Daucus carota sativa

Carrots do well under lights if you plant one of the short varieties. Long carrots don't develop well if their root tips collide with the bottom of the container. Even for short carrots, use a container at least four inches deep and preferably five or six inches. Plant the seed with great restraint and thin the seedlings to one and one-half inches apart while they're still quite small. It's best to cut extra plants off with a small scissors; pulling close-growing seedlings may disturb the roots of those you want to keep. Expect your carrot harvest about seven weeks after planting.

Chinese Cabbage

Brassica chinensis: loose leaf

Brassica pekinensis: solid heads

Chinese cabbage grows tender, crisp, and delicious under lights. It does not suffer transplanting in good grace and has a tendency to bolt to seed if subjected to freezing temperatures. Otherwise, it is an excellent choice for light gardening. We've just polished off a tub full of it, tossed with onion, carrot, and Jerusalem artichoke slices in a vinegar and oil dressing, with a good-sized tuft of thyme snipped over. The salad was the perfect foil for a dish of chili, especially on a winter day when no green thing was to be seen outdoors.

The best container is a five-inch-deep pan of some sort, with about six inches of space between plants. A weekly dose of fertilizer will promote the crisp leafy growth you want. You might even decide to put a pot of Chinese cabbage on display as a houseplant . . . it's that handsome.

Beets

Beta vulgaris

Beets will surprise you, too. They won't grow into great thumping garden-style specimens, but wouldn't a rosy bunch of tender baby beets be just as welcome on a chill February day? Plant the seed in a clay pot or deep dishpan. Beet seeds should be covered with a one-eighth-inch layer of soil and firmed well with your hand or a block of wood. Since what we call a beet seed is really an aggregate of several seeds, each of which will probably sprout, you may have some thinning to do. Allow two to three inches between plants. Beets are a two-in-one vegetable; the leafy tops are delicious steamed or creamed or (when young) torn into a tossed salad.

Spinach

Spinacea oleracea

Spinach likes cool weather and short days, so keep the temperature in the fifties or low sixties and limit light to sixteen hours. You can allow seedlings to grow two inches apart, thinning as they grow to an eventual three- to four-inch spacing. The weeded-out seedlings make a lovely addition to the soup pot.

Parsley
Petroselinum hortense

After several years of doggedly digging up parsley in the fall only to have it languish indoors, I've concluded that the best way to raise indoor parsley is to start from seed in the fall. Parsley does well on a sunny windowsill if you don't have a light set-up.

Germination is slow – two weeks at best, and often three – so be sure to keep the flat moist all that time. Parsley is worth the wait, though, when you can surprise your family with a fresh green sprig of it on their breakfast eggs. Young parsley seedlings, those that have just sprouted their scalloped-edge leaves, transplant well. Space them about three inches apart in a clay pot and snip at will once they begin to branch out. Later, parsley develops a deep taproot which makes successful transplanting difficult, but you can set your winter-grown plants out in the garden in spring. Just knock them out of the pot and give them a respectable hole lined with a welcome mat of compost.

Chives
Allium schoenoprasum

A pot of chives started from seed or brought in from the garden will thrive on a sunny windowsill. Keep several pots of chives and harvest them alternately all winter.

Thyme
Thymus vulgaris

Although a perennial, thyme has such an unassuming manner that it is easily lost in the garden. I usually pot up several plants in a six-inch pot and keep it under lights or on the sunny windowsill. Put some extra gravel in the bottom of the pot and an extra shake of sharp sand or Perlite in the planting mix to assure good drainage.

Thyme grows slowly and its leaves are tiny but a pinch of it makes a real difference in a stew or soup.

Dill
Anethum graveolens

Fresh-snipped dill with your winter fish dinners makes it all worthwhile. Your potted dill won't be likely to form flowers and seeds like that you plant in the garden, but the feathery aromatic leaves are just what you want when a meal needs a little extra zip. Try some in potato soup too. Dill germinates slowly; it may take two weeks. Keep the soil moist and space the seedlings two inches apart. You can begin cutting the tops when they're about three inches high. Chop them finely to release all the aromatic oil.

Tomatoes
Lycopersicon esculentum

Tomatoes are trickier to raise indoors than the greens and roots I've already mentioned, but many gardeners have found it possible to harvest fruit from plants grown under lights. If you are sufficiently determined, you can too. For your first efforts, choose one of the small-fruited varieties. Most seed companies offer at least one kind. You might want to use one of the special plant growth-enhancing fluorescent tubes to encourage flowering.

Tomatoes need warm growing temperatures of 70 to 75 degrees F., weekly fertilizing and *lots* of light. To fruit well, they must receive 2,500 foot candles of light, in contrast to lettuce, which needs only 1,000 foot candles of light for leaf production. In order to provide this amount of light, you'll need a group of four to six 40-watt tubes. Reflective metal or flat-white painted surfaces surrounding the plants will help to increase the amount of light available to them. Tomatoes, by the way, are self-pollinating, so you should not need to worry about transferring pollen from one blossom to another. Each blossom pollinates itself. You can help things along, though, by jiggling the plants when they're in full bloom to duplicate the effect of wind on outdoor plants. Stake the fruiting plants, for even small fruits can be heavy.

II. Flowers, Herbs, and Teas

Flowers in the Soup
Grow Perennial Flowers from Seed
Growing Wildflowers from Seed
Grow Your Own Teas
A Traditional Medicinal Garden

Flowers in the Soup

Day Lily

The use of flowers in cookery is an ancient tradition, but one that has oddly enough been little practiced in recent years. Could it have something to do with the facile separation of mind/body, pleasure/duty, beauty/usefulness that has, until recently, afflicted our culture? There are hopeful signs that this is changing, that we've begun to see that such rigid categorizing doesn't work. Mind and body are one; whole. The line between work and play is not the neat cleavage we had been accustomed to assume. And, just as there is beauty in a well-designed functional object, so too there is no reason why we should not make use of beautiful things in new/old ways when they serve our purposes.

The flowers we plant in our gardens as ornamentals today were often grown especially for culinary purposes in centuries gone by. Extracts of certain blooms – notably roses and orange blossoms – were used 200 to 300 years ago as extensively as we use vanilla today. Early-eighteenth-century cookbooks offer recipes for soups and salads that include marigold, cowslip, and violet flowers along with strawberry leaves, lettuce, and spinach.

Flowers can be good food. If the idea of eating blossoms still seems strange to you, consider that when you have broccoli for dinner, what you're eating is a tightly packed mass of flower buds.

From there, it's not really a very big jump to planting a few calendulas for cooking, growing some violets and day lilies especially for their flowers, or collecting the fragrant petals of the rose.

Naturally, you wouldn't use just any flower to embellish your meals. Not everything that blooms is good to eat. The flower foods I'm about to describe *have* been proven safe to eat, though, and they're wholesome and tasty as well. Just be sure to use clean, fresh blossoms that are free of disease and chemical sprays, and don't substitute other flowers not on this list unless you know that they are edible. (The following are not the only edible flowers, just the ones with which I am familiar.)

For your first culinary flower garden, I'd recommend planting a few of the following time-tested favorites. Perhaps the sense of daring engendered by eating fried flowers will give you an inkling of the adventuresome spirit shown by those first few hardy souls who were brave enough to try the strange new potatoes and tomatoes brought to Europe from the New World.

Borage
Borago officinalis

Borage has been useful in the kitchen since Roman times. The star-shaped flowers, borne in profusion on the two-foot-tall plants, are a beautiful clear blue – the color of forget-me-nots and Virginia blue-bells, which are both fairly close relatives.

Use borage blossoms to garnish a cool drink or an upended cup custard. Float them in the punch bowl or, better yet, freeze them in an ice ring or in individual cubes of ice.

In Victorian days, borage blossoms were candied by dipping them in egg white and sprinkling them with sugar. That's gilding the lily, though. The blossoms are startlingly pretty just as they are, and all that sugar does no one good.

If you're short of salad ingredients, borage leaves are good to eat too. Chop them finely, though, because they're rather hairy.

Although an annual, borage self-sows so readily that you're likely to have it around for years after you make your first planting. Sow the seeds a week or so before your last expected spring frost and thin the plants to stand ten inches apart. You can get away with trans-planting young borage seedlings but more fully developed plants are difficult to transplant successfully.

Site is more important than soil for borage; it thrives in many kinds of soil but prefers a dry, sunny location.

Calendula
Calendula officinalis

The calendula, or pot marigold, as it is sometimes called, has a long and honorable history of culinary use. It was, in fact, a staple house-hold medicine in medieval times, when the blossoms were con-sidered an effective treatment for a wide variety of ailments. It ap-pears in eighteenth-century cookbooks as an ingredient in soups, stews, salads, and meat dishes. In many peasant cultures the world over, cooking with calendula blossoms has never gone out of style. The bright yellow flowers are often used to color butter and give a rich golden shade to noodles and egg dishes. It is an excellent homegrown substitute for saffron, which is less easy to obtain and therefore quite expensive. While the typical rich-musty saffron flavor is missing in the mild tasting calendula petals, they impart an appetizing color.

I like to sprinkle a handful of calendula petals into tossed salad, soup, stew, and rice dishes. They contribute more color than flavor, but they look festive and add some natural vitamins and minerals. Just pluck the petals from the flower head and discard the central button. The petals may be eaten either raw or cooked. Many country people dry a supply to last over the winter. The dried petals may be stirred into most any recipe, from cooked cereal to muffins to fish chowder. Try using them instead of the saffron in that traditional Pennsylvania Dutch dish, chicken pot pie, or in your next paella.

Calendulas are easy to raise from seed. For early June bloom, sow seeds indoors in March and set out plants a foot apart in late April or early May. They don't mind light frost. In fact, the plant prefers to keep cool, from germination of the seed, which sprouts best at temperatures between 60 and 65 degrees F., right through to the time of bloom. Calendulas put on a good show during the mild days of early summer, before the weather gets hot. They look a bit straggly during the hotter days of July and August but come into their own again in September and October as the original plants form new buds, especially if they've been cut back at the end of the first period of bloom.

Calendula is an annual that grows to a height of fifteen to eighteen inches, with daisy-like orange and yellow flowers. It self-sows readily and volunteers from unclipped spring blooms that went to seed will brighten the fall garden.

Day Lily

Hemerocallis fulva – wild

H. flava – cultivated

Day-lily blossoms are everyday fare in the Orient. Either the bud or the day-old spent blossom may be cooked. The flavor is mild and good, not unlike green beans. Braised with beef, batter-fried, or steamed and buttered, the day-lily flower is a delicacy that most people enjoy at first taste. The first time you serve them, simply steam the flowers in a covered pot for about five minutes. In this way, you'll discover their true flavor, and then you can go on to add them to soups, stews, and casseroles and stir them into your favorite

Oriental-style dinner along with thin slivers of meat, peppers, onions, and a sweet/sour sauce.

Orange day lilies of the common garden variety often grow unbidden in old perennial borders and even wild, blooming in June and July along the roadside or around the crumbling stone cellar holes of burned-down farmhouses. Newer hybrids, which include subtle gradations of yellow, maroon, orange, and peach, extend the blooming season through August.

Day lilies will grow almost anywhere, except in deep shade or swampy ground, as long as they have decent average soil. They are hardy, disease-free, and not preyed upon by any important insect pests. Indeed, they are one of the easiest perennials you can grow. To start, plant a root or division from an established clump. Or, for a somewhat more adventurous approach, grow some plants from seed. You can sow day-lily seed in a cold frame in the fall and transplant the seedlings to a nursery row when they germinate in the spring, or you can get an early indoor start by sowing the seed in flats in February. They'll germinate in two weeks. Set them out in the garden around the time of your last frost. Gradually thin the seedlings until they stand two feet apart by the end of their first summer. By their second summer, the long, thin, sword-shaped leaves will have grown to full size – a bushy clump three feet tall. Seed-grown plants can be depended on to bloom by the third year; some will even bloom by the second summer. Once established, they need little care except to divide the clumps if they become crowded. Don't mow down the foliage after bloom; the plants need those green leaves to nourish their roots.

Elderberry Flower
Sambucus canadensis

The elderberry is a bushy shrub that grows in damp places and produces purple-black edible berries in late summer. (See page 101 for notes on elderberry culture.) The bushes bear quantities of saucer-flat, white flower clusters (umbels) in late spring and early summer. These blossom heads, also called elder-blow, form the basis for an unusual countryman's treat . . . elder-blow pancakes or fritters. This is not the sort of dish you'd serve twice a week; most devotees, as far as I know, consider a serving or two a season to be their just due. For if you pick *all* the blossoms, of course, you'll have no berries. (Some folks pick their yearly share of blossoms from remote wild bushes, which often have their berries stripped by birds before foragers can get to them.)

Nevertheless, elder-blow fritters are a special seasonal treat and one that you owe it to yourself to try. Simply make up a batch of your favorite pancake batter. We like a mixture of equal parts of buckwheat, soy, and whole wheat flours. Dip each flower head in batter and fry it in an inch of oil until it's crisp and brown. Drizzle honey or maple syrup over the fritters. Sigh. Delicious.

Marigold
Tagetes minuta, lucida, etc.

Marigold blossoms may be used interchangeably with those of the calendula. They are somewhat more pungent and come in a wider color range of rust, yellow, orange, and even near-white. The petals are not quite as readily detachable from the flower as those of the calendula, but you can always snip them off if they don't pull readily. Try adding three tablespoons of marigold petals to a six-egg omelet. Or stir some into a lamb stew. Or include one-fourth cup of the petals in a vegetable chowder made with cooked potato, onion, celery, parsley, and one quart of hot milk.

Marigold seed is available in a wide range of plant sizes, from dwarf (six to eight inches) to bushy mid-size (two to two and one-half feet) to tall (three to four feet). For earliest bloom, plant seed indoors in March and set plants out in May. They are more frost-tender than calendulas. Or sow seed right in the garden row a week or so before your last expected frost. Space tall varieties eighteen inches apart, mid-size twelve to fifteen inches apart, and dwarf kinds six inches apart. When transplanting, set the plants somewhat more deeply than they were in their pots or flats. They do best in full sun, are not particular as to soil, and hardly ever host insect pests.

Nasturtium
Tropaeolum majus – climbing;
Timinus – bush form; *T. nanum* – dwarf

The bright, clear colors of the nasturtium have a place on the dinner table as well as along the garden path. Not only the flowers but also the leaves and seeds are fairly well-known, if not widely used, table fare. Surprise your family this evening by serving nasturtium blossoms stuffed with chicken salad! More conventional uses for both flowers and leaves of this good-natured plant include cooking them in soup and tossing them in salad. I like the color and peppery tang this flower food gives to mixtures of bland ingredients – rice dishes, leaf lettuce salads, chicken soup. As with other flower foods or unfamiliar fare, start small by snipping just a flower or two into a dish you're preparing, and work up to the proportion that seems most pleasing.

Some of the most spectacular beds of nasturtiums I've ever seen were growing in what looked like pure sand near a weather-beaten oceanfront cottage in Maine – an extreme example of the gardening truism that nasturtiums bloom best in poor soil. They bloom well, but not outstandingly, at the edge of my kitchen garden, which has pretty good soil. Full sun and well-drained ground will also promote good bloom. Nasturtiums have tender, sappy stems, so they don't transplant well. Plant the seeds about four inches apart right in the garden after the danger of frost has passed. Thin seedlings to stand a foot apart.

In the fall, I often gather an armful of nasturtium leaves and blossoms to bring in when frost is predicted, because it is one of the first plants to keel over when night frost strikes.

Orange Blossoms

Citrus sinensis – common orange

C. taitensis – Otaheite orange

Although oranges prosper as a commercial crop only in Florida, California, and a narrow corridor of southwest Arizona, a dwarf species, the Otaheite orange, is often grown as a greenhouse or indoor plant in the North. The small oranges it bears rate rather low on the flavor scale, but the blossoms are fragrant and good. You might try glazing two cups of cooked, sliced beets with two tablespoons of melted butter into which you've stirred one tablespoon of orange flower petals. Or combine two tablespoons of petals with two cups of cooked rice, a handful of raisins, one-fourth cup of orange juice, and garnish with one-fourth cup of toasted chopped almonds. Include a few of the flowers in duck stuffing, rice pudding, or ham loaf, and use them to garnish drinks and salads.

As pot plants, these little trees need full sun, good rich soil that is well drained (put at least one inch of pebbles on the bottom of the pot before putting the plant into it) and a steady supply of water. Don't let them wilt. Rotate the pot a quarter turn each week to keep plant growth even.

If you are ever able to gather enough petals, you can make orange-flower-water by the same method used to make rosewater. (See the next entry on the rose.) This gets to be a bit precious for a one-person kitchen crew, though, unless you have several orange trees in your yard. Most of us will have to content ourselves with an occasional jar of orange-water. A steady supply of this delicacy was one of those niceties that was possible only in years gone by when the servant staff outnumbered the members of the household. Still, I like to imagine the medieval castle kitchen, its dark corners redolent of essence of orange or rose steeping in a kettle by the open fire, while the cook and his assistants sift through fresh-picked piles of blossoms heaped on the massive oak table.

Rose
Rosa

Since well before Elizabethan times, rose blooms have been used to add a note of fragrance, color, and flavor to all kinds of foods from pies to soups to custards to vegetables. Try layering some rose petals in a fruit compote, using rosewater to season apple pie, flavoring custard or pudding with rosewater instead of vanilla, blending dried rose petals and chives into cream cheese for a cracker spread, glazing cooked whole baby carrots with rose butter (made by beating two teaspoons of rosewater into one pound of butter.)

To make rosewater, gather one pound of fresh rose petals, preferably from one of the old extra-fragrant varieties. The petals will have more fragrance on a warm, sunny, dry day. Measure three cups of the petals, cover them with water, and simmer gently for forty minutes. Drain off the water into another pan, add another three cups of petals to the water, and cook these for forty minutes. Continue in this way to cook the rest of the fresh petals, three cups at a time, in the increasingly concentrated rose liquor, without adding any more water, unless the mixture is in danger of boiling dry. Filter the rose concentrate and keep it, covered, in the refrigerator, or freeze in small amounts, as in ice-cube trays.

If you want to begin a little rose garden, here are a few pointers: Roses need full sun, acid, well-drained soil (pH 5 to 6), and good air circulation. Replace part of the soil from the planting hole with a generous shovelful of well-rotted manure when setting out the bushes. Plant them at least one foot – better two feet – away from nearby buildings for better circulation of air. Spacing depends on variety, but three feet between plants is usual. Plant the bushes either spring or fall, unless you have exceptionally early and cold winters, in which case spring planting is best. Where winters are severe (under 10 degrees F.) the bushes should be protected by mounding up soil around them and covering the frozen ground with a mulch of hay or leaves, which is sometimes held in place with stakes and wire or burlap.

Squash Blossoms
Cucurbita maxima; C. moschata

Zuni Indians, and presumably other tribes as well, often picked the male blossoms from their squash plants to add to soup. No gardener would deliberately denude food plants of their fruit-bearing female blossoms and thus spoil the crop, when all but a few of the male pollinator blooms may safely be eaten and enjoyed without interfering with vegetable production. Nature provides prodigiously for the dissemination of pollen. Male blossoms appear at the end of a relatively long stem, and there is no swelling at the base of the bud. Female blossoms often (but not always) have shorter stems and a swollen area – often an actual tiny fruit – appears at the base of the blossom.

To serve squash blossoms in soup, add them during the last five minutes of cooking. The blossoms are also sometimes dipped in batter and fried.

Sunflower
Helianthus anuus

The sunflowers we grow for their robust, cheerful appearance and tasty seeds were interrupted in the blossoming stage by early American colonists and their sixteenth-century English forebears. The old way with sunflowers was to cook the flower bud until tender and either pickle it or serve it with a lemon-butter sauce. You might want to try this with one of those sunflower plants that grows many small three- to six-inch heads. (See page 154 for sunflower growing suggestions.)

Violet
Viola sororia – common purple
V. eriocarpa – yellow

Many of the violets I pick for eating never get as far as the kitchen; they make a piquant lavender nibble that can be gathered along the way on an early spring walk. The blossoms that remain when my rambles have brought me back to my front door will grace the dinner table as a garnish for our salad of early green garden lettuce.

Wild violets are not hard to find. They survive transplanting quite well and often spread to form a ground cover in their new home. If possible, take some of the soil in which they've been growing and pat it around the roots when replanting them. Give them a spot with part shade, not too dry, and try tucking them in rocky pockets to keep their roots cool. The purple, white, or yellow native violets may be eaten, but not the unrelated dogtooth violet.

The blossoms are not only arrestingly beautiful, they are also a good source of vitamin C. According to studies run at Penn State University at the suggestion of wild foods expert Euell Gibbons, and tabulated in his book *Stalking the Healthful Herbs,* 100 grams of violet blossoms contain 150 mg. of vitamin C.

In addition to serving the fresh leaves and blossoms in salads and other dishes, Gibbons concocted a violet syrup by cooking violets with lemon and sugar and made violet jam by blending the petals with a boiled pectin/water mixture.

Medieval and Victorian cooks, who may have forgotten that the culinary and medicinal use of plain, unadorned violet blossoms dates back at least as far as the writings of Homer and Virgil, often outdid themselves by dipping the individual blossoms in beaten egg white and then in sugar, drying the confections in a warm place, and using them to garnish equally improbable storied puddings and cakes. Since the blossoms have real food value, though, in addition to the decorative effect, I prefer to use them in wholesome dishes in which they can make a positive contribution to my family's health. To vary the violets-in-salad routine, you might want to try embedding freshly picked violet blossoms in a gelatin salad made with lemonade or a light-colored herb tea as a base, along with cucumber slices, chopped chives, and super-thin shavings of spring radishes.

Flower Tips

1. Pick flowers around noon on a sunny, dry day if possible.
2. To dry flowers, spread them on a sheet-covered screen or large piece of cardboard in a hot, dry, dark, well-ventilated place. For best results, individual petals should not touch each other. Dry violets whole. Composite flowers like calendula or marigold may be dried more quickly if petals are plucked off.
3. To make flower vinegar, pour vinegar over one to two cups of dried flower petals in a glass jar, enamel pan, or earthenware crock. Keep in a warm place for one to two weeks. Strain the liquid and store it in a cool spot.
4. Dried blossoms may be powdered by grinding them with a mortar and pestle.
5. Check your own favorite recipes to find familiar dishes that are good candidates for flower embellishment, using these tried-and-true flower varieties.

Grow Perennial Flowers from Seed

Columbine

Perennial flowers that increase as the years go by are one of the great pleasures of gardening. By growing them from seed, you can obtain plants in colors and varieties that would be difficult if not impossible to buy. And rather than content yourself with a few lone hardy flowers spotted among the early bulbs, you can enjoy a whole drift of them. Some will even bloom the first year from seed. Of the many perennials available for starting from scratch, I'll describe here some that I have grown and found satisfying and adaptable. These include spring- and summer-blooming plants. Together, they'll form the basis of a colorful perennial bed . . . yours by next year if you start this spring.

Balloonflower
Platycodon grandiflorum

Balloonflower is especially easy to grow from seed. Start plants indoors in February or March or in the garden in May. Germination takes a week or more inside, closer to three weeks outside. A long-lived perennial, platycodon self-sows readily. Its one puzzling characteristic is its late appearance in spring. The leaves don't begin to grow until May, so you may want to mark the spot where they grow to prevent inadvertent rooting out of the plant when setting out other plants. Balloonflower is fun to watch; the purple bud opens from a hollow balloon to a star-shaped flower. Average height is eighteen to thirty inches. Space plants about fifteen inches apart. Tall specimens may need to be staked. Mature plants form a taproot and transplant poorly, so seedlings should be planted out where you want them to grow as soon as they have two or three sets of true leaves and the weather is frost-free.

Blanketflower
Gaillardia

A favorite of the casual gardener, blanketflower plants are quite hardy, self-sow readily, and bloom even in poor soil and dry weather. Red, orange, yellow, copper, bronze, and deep maroon shades on both solid colors and concentric circles blend, in a bed or row, to give the impression of a rich-hued Indian blanket.

I planted gaillardia indoors in flats in March, keeping the flats in a warm place (about 80 degrees F.) for the three weeks necessary for germination. You can also plant the seed in the open ground any time after April. My plants, set out twelve inches apart in full sun, bloomed the first year, but later summer sowings might not bloom until the following year.

Columbine
Aquilegia

With their airy, long-spurred dancing blooms, columbines bloom in my garden during May and June. Colors of the cultivated strains range from rose to red, yellow, cream, pink, white, and blue. Some will be bicolors. Old-fashioned short-spurred columbines are rose, purple, or white. They have heavier foliage and somewhat coarser blossoms but are lovely and dependable. One white columbine I raised from seed in my first garden had double blooms, but when I breathlessly called the Horticultural Society about it I was told that the flowers would no doubt be sterile, since pollinating insects have difficulty finding their way in.

Plant seeds indoors in February or March, or in an outdoor seedbed during May or June. For best results, chill the seeds at a temperature of 40 degrees F. for five days to break their dormancy before you plant them. Just press them into the flat of moist soil; do not cover them. Warm temperatures (between 70 and 80 degrees F.) will promote germination, which takes two to three weeks. The little seedlings with their wiry stems will give you some hint of their future colors when you develop an eye for the subtle differences in leaf color. Pale-leafed plants usually have white blooms. Those that bloom red or purple will often have a deeper green or even purplish leaf color.

Columbines grown from seed bloom the year after planting. They grow slowly and do not transplant well once they've sent down a central taproot, so young seedlings should be planted in their permanent places when they have two or three sets of leaves, if possible. Space them fifteen to eighteen inches apart; dwarf varieties which grow only fifteen inches high rather than the usual two to three feet may be planted nine to twelve inches apart. Columbines like good soil and ample moisture. They will bloom in part shade or full sun. The only problem I've ever had with columbines has been unsightly pale serpentine markings on some leaves, caused by the leaf miner. The best cure is prevention; cultivating around the plant early in the season disturbs the leaf miner's life cycle.

Day Lily
Hemerocallis

The day lily's proper name, translated from the Greek, means 'beautiful for a day.' While the blossoming period is unusually generous, usually two months in midsummer (July and August), the individual blooms fade at the end of each day, and more buds open to replace them on the following day. The long, slender leaves spray out over the lawn in a graceful manner, and thus the plant improves the landscape even when not in bloom.

Plants mature in about a year and a half. Some will bloom the year after seed planting; others not until the third year. Sow the seed indoors at the beginning of March. At 70 degrees F. the seeds will germinate in three weeks. Transplant the seedlings to a nursery row in May and move them to their permanent location, spaced two feet apart, in fall or early spring the following year. Seed may also be sown in the cold frame in fall, to germinate in early spring. It is best to avoid putting fresh manure around the plants. Day lilies do well in ordinary garden soil in a sunny location. The long wait until blossoming time is more than offset by the variety, hardiness, and longevity of the day-lily plant.

Many sumptuous bright and subtle shades of the rose, yellow, salmon, copper, and maroon trumpet-shaped flowers – some with extra markings – are available in seed mixtures for those who, like me, can't resist the lure of the unknown. You might even want to save seed from named varieties of day lilies already growing in your garden. Simply collect the mature dry pods before they drop their seeds and proceed as described above.

If you're feeling even more adventurous, try doing your own plant breeding. The day lily is a good flower for your first efforts in this direction. First find the anthers, the thickened pollen-covered tips of the long, slender stamens. Each lily has six stamens. In the center of the flowers, surrounded by stamens, you'll find the tubular style, leading to the ovary, with the pollen-receptive stigma at its outer tip. In order to form seed, the flower must be pollinated; pollen must be transferred from the anthers to the stigma, where it will start its own journey that culminates in the development of ripened seed. Pinch off one of the stamens from a good parent flower and rub the pollen off onto the stigma of your other parent flower. Watch carefully for seedpod formation. Be sure to record what you've done and label the pollinated flower. You might, for example, want to transfer pollen from an early-blooming flower to another early bloomer in hopes of getting seed that will grow into an extra-early blooming day lily. Or you might play around with different colors, just to see what you'll get.

Delphinium

Delphinium is an aristocrat. Tall, stately, bearing masses of true blue, violet, white, or rose blooms, the plants will bloom the first summer from seed started indoors in winter. Bloom will be heavier in succeeding years, and if cut back after early summer bloom, many plants will blossom again in the fall.

Unless seed is very fresh, it will need chilling to persuade it to break dormancy. Freeze the seed for twenty-four hours before planting. January or February is a good time to plant the seeds indoors in flats. Soil temperature of 55 to 60 degrees F. promotes good germination; higher temperatures tend to induce dormancy. Plant the seed one-eighth inch deep and keep the flat moist until you see that seeds have sprouted. Expect seedlings about three weeks after planting. Keep the seedlings cool; 60 degrees F. during the day and 50 degrees F. at night is ideal.

I set my seedlings out in late May in a well-drained sunny spot enriched by compost. Allow eighteen to twenty-four inches between plants. Delphiniums like lime and do well on relatively sandy soil, but they must be well fed. Be sure to stake the plants, especially the four- to five-foot-tall Pacific Giants, but even the two-foot dwarf varieties, for the heavy flower stalk often breaks in the wind if unsupported. Plants infested with cyclamen mite will have blackened, poorly formed buds and deformed leaves. Dust with rotenone to kill the mites. Another problem sometimes encountered by delphinium growers is bacterial leaf spot – odd-shaped black patches on the leaves. Once present, leaf spot can't be cured, but it can be prevented by cutting off all dead leaves and stems in the fall to eliminate winter hiding places for the bacteria that cause the disease.

Flax

Linum perenne

Flax is one of the easiest flowering perennials to grow from seed. The blossoms are a lovely clear true blue, borne on soft ferny foliage that fills in well in the bulb garden. My planting of these beauties has been casual in the extreme. I simply scatter the small black seeds liberally among the spring bulbs in early April, scratch them into the soil, and then watch for the delicate seedlings, which are almost like asparagus seedlings, but with blunt 'needles' and gray-green color. Flax self-sows readily and transplants fairly well while seedlings are small. Plants should be thinned to at least a four-inch spacing. They bloom continuously for two months in June and July and usually blossom the same year they're planted.

Hollyhocks

Althaea rosea

In the dooryard gardens of Provincetown and Williamsburg, by railroad tracks, in small-town backyards, hollyhocks open their ice-cream-colored blossoms to the bees. I'm especially fond of them, I guess, because they once helped me to transform a rented house into a home. The seeds I planted in a front yard of our temporary Wisconsin residence grew into six-foot plants that curtained the front window with shades of apricot, rose, cream, yellow, and pink the following summer. In the same town, I discovered a whole backyard full of hollyhock blooms, a solid block of them, all colors . . . a hollyhock lover's paradise!

Hollyhock seeds germinate best in cool soil, around 60 degrees F., so plant them early, in April or May, in full sun, right in the open ground. Seedlings may be transplanted, but only when quite small. It is much better to simply plant the seeds where they are to grow. Thin to a fifteen- to eighteen-inch spacing. Hollyhocks will bloom in June of the year following planting. They are very hardy and usually immune to insect damage. From a plant bearing deep rose blooms I've collected seed that grew into plants that bloomed in a whole palette of pastel colors, plus deep maroon. Once I have a stand of hollyhocks, I like to play Johnny Appleseed and collect the seed to toss in waste places, on hedgerows, and out-of-the-way corners where their blooms may surprise and delight travelers.

Primrose
Primula

Primroses include some of the most varied and colorful flowers that can be grown. This April-blooming perennial with its crinkled leathery leaves and bright clear flower heads comes in almost any color you could want: yellow, rose, cream, lavender, pink, salmon, white, purple, carmine. One of my favorite plantings is in my friend Harriet's garden where primroses blooming under a clump of birch-trees make a charming early spring view from the kitchen window. In my own garden, primroses nestle among the daffodils and tulips, and again between dwarf white azalea bushes in an eastern exposure. The plants I've raised from seed seem to be hardier than those I purchased at a nursery.

Primrose seed is very slow to germinate. Some kinds take as long as two years. The seed is fine and needs plenty of light and air in order to germinate, as well as a period of freezing to break dormancy. February or early March is a good time to plant the seeds. Sphagnum moss makes a good seedbed. Saturate the moss and press the seeds into the surface, but do not cover them. Then set the flat outdoors in a protected place where it will not be raked by animals or flooded by rain. It should not be allowed to dry out. After several weeks of outdoor cold, bring the flat inside and expose it to light, even though no seedlings have appeared. Germination occurs most completely at around 70 degrees F.

The first seedlings will appear in about six weeks and stragglers will continue to pop up well into the summer if you keep the flat moist and well lit. The tiny crinkly leafed seedlings are delicate. They should be transplanted to good rich potting soil as soon as possible after germination, and given plenty of moisture with good drainage.

Soil for primroses should be rich, well supplied with humus, and well drained. Part shade suits them very well. Hot steady sun and dry spots should be reserved for other plants. In my experience, an eastern exposure with dappled shade from tall old trees seems to foster good primrose growth. Set the plants about ten inches apart. The foliage will occasionally die back in late summer but the plants should reappear the following spring if their moisture supply has been adequate. Alternate thawing and freezing can damage prim-roses severely by tearing vital feeder roots. Protect them over winter by mulching with straw or evergreen branches after the ground has frozen. Primroses grown from seed will bloom the year after planting. When you see the colors, you'll probably find yourself completely captivated by these bright early spring bloomers.

Shasta Daisy

Chrysanthemum maximum

Daisies are a must in summer bouquets, and the hardy shastas are easy to start and faithful about returning. They are available in fourteen-inch dwarf form, eighteen- to twenty-four-inch hybrids in various colors, and the more usual two- to three-foot-tall yellow-centered white daisy. All are tolerant of cold winters and appreciative of full sun and good drainage. Soil need not be especially rich but reasonably fertile soil will produce the best daisy display.

Start seed in flats indoors in late winter, or in a nursery row in mid spring. Keep them on the cool side. Shasta daisy plants germinate best at 60 to 65 degrees F. Light promotes their germination, so don't cover the seed, just press it into the damp soil. Expect to see seedlings three weeks after planting. The young plants may be transplanted to the garden around the time of the last frost. They often bloom the first year. When weeding, watch for volunteer shastas from seed dropped by mature plants.

Several basic principles apply to the care of all perennial flowers. For one thing, most of these plants have extensive root systems, so it is important to dig a large enough hole to easily accept the roots without crowding. Also, winter mulch should be applied *after* the soil freezes to more effectively prevent heaving of the plant during winter thaws. In addition, perennial plants, with the exception of flax and hollyhocks which are rather difficult to keep groomed, should not be allowed to go to seed. Conserve the plant's strength by snipping off all spent blooms.

There are all kinds of possibilities in a packet of flower seeds. If you want a perennial border, or some bright color in the garden to follow the spring bulbs, or some plants to sell to help support your gardening mania, perhaps this is the adventure you'd like to put first on your list. Even if you only add one new variety of perennial each year, in a very few years you could have a border massed with the shifting patchwork of succeeding multicolored blooms . . . and all from an envelope of seed.

Growing Wildflowers from Seed

Jack-in-the-Pulpit

When we were living in Philadelphia, our naturalist neighbors once returned a pie pan to me filled to overflowing with wild plants. It was one of the nicest reciprocal gifts I've ever received. There in a shallow ten-inch vessel was a world in miniature: yellow violets, a mayapple umbrella, silky wild ginger leaves, little blue-flowered Jacob's ladder plants, hepatica with its Dresden blossoms, tiny hummocks of moss, nudgings of uncurling ferns. Dense with bloom and textural variety, the scene could have come from a Botticelli painting. It was the start of my first wildflower garden.

In all the places we've lived since, in small towns, in suburbs, on rural routes, I've managed to plant at least a handkerchief-sized wildflower corner. This is not as hard to do in town as one might suppose, because every house has its shady side, and that is where many wild plants do well. Those that do prefer full sun, the meadow flowers, are usually tall, sturdy, and easy to grow.

It took me quite some time, though, to entertain the thought of growing wildflowers from seed, even though some of the plants I'd introduced into my wild corner, especially the wild geranium and columbine, were self-sowing freely. We are accustomed to thinking of starting with plants when growing wildflowers, if indeed we think of working with them at all. Wildflowers lack the commercial clout of plants like corn and cotton, soybeans and tomatoes, so comparatively few studies have been made on raising them from seed. The important work has largely been done by dedicated amateurs, often allied with one of the voluntary plant societies, especially the New England Wildflower Society, The American Horticultural Society, and The American Fern Society.

Unlike petunias, marigolds, and other common bedding plants, most wildflowers need relatively specific conditions. They have, in general, a fairly narrow margin of tolerance for more sun, acid, moisture, or other deviations from their ideal natural growing conditions. Fitting the plant to the site, then, becomes part of the adventure of growing wildflowers.

Why grow wildflowers from seed? It is much easier to successfully transplant many wild plants in the seedling stage rather than as mature plants. Starting from seed will give you many plants, perhaps even enough to give away or sell. You will also have plenty of plants for experimentation; by planting several wildflower seedlings in each of three or four locations, you will discover where the plants will thrive best. Furthermore, in working with the plants from the very beginning you will learn more about how they grow and what they need, so that you'll be better prepared to nurture them properly.

There are some plants, like trailing arbutus, which should *only* be obtained by planting seed, or by layering established plants. (To propagate a plant by layering, nick the underside of a branch or stem lightly with a knife, press the abraded stem into soft ground next to the parent plant, and cover firmly with more soil, held down by a stone. Leave several leaves exposed. Roots will form on the buried stem, usually within a year. When enough roots have grown on the new plant it may be removed from the parent plant and transplanted.) Arbutus is so scarce that it should never be dug from the wild, especially since it hardly ever transplants successfully, depending as it does on a very precise relationship between its roots and certain specific soil fungi. Sad to say, arbutus plants offered for sale may have been dug from the wild; I would never purchase such plants and thus support further depredations unless I was certain that the grower had personally propagated the plants – no easy undertaking.

Many of our native plants have been pushed into a corner by the wholesale leveling of woods, draining of swamps, and paving of meadows that has accompanied both residential and commercial building expansion. Overpicking of shy growers like lady's slippers, fringed gentian, and trailing arbutus has also endangered their survival. The contribution you make by starting new, viable pockets of native wild bloomers could be more far-reaching than you might suspect when you set those first seedlings out under the evergreen tree in your yard.

Seed may be obtained by collecting it from wild plants you find on hikes and trips, purchasing from commercial seedsmen, and trading through a seed exchange or special-interest plant society. Collecting seed from the wild can be an adventure in itself. Unless you know the area very well, you're not likely to find it possible to just go to the woods, pocket the seed, and head straight home. First, you'll need to locate the plants and see them in bloom. Spend some time observing the surroundings of the plant from which you want to gather seed. What kinds of trees does it grow under? A setting of oaks, laurel, rhododendron, and evergreens indicates acid soil. Does it bloom in sun or dappled shade? (Southern plants that require shade in their native habitat will often thrive in partial sun in the North. The reverse is true, too.) Is the ground dry, sandy, rocky, moist, soggy? What kind of rocks, if any, predominate – limestone, ironstone, shale, granite? It may take several excursions to catch the plants at the seeding stage. In the case of gentians, spring beauties, jack-in-the-pulpit, bloodroot, and other plants that are sometimes overshadowed by their weedy neighbors before they've ripened seed, you might want to mark the plant with a stake or rock circle so that you can find it again. Many wildflower plants like jewelweed, violet, and wild geranium project their ripe seeds a surprising distance from the parent plant. For that reason, it's a good idea to tie a small cloth or perforated paper bag over the ripening seed head to catch the seeds at just the right time.

When collecting wild seed, take only a small portion of seed from any one group of plants. Never collect all or most of the seed from a small population of plants that is the only one of its kind in the area. Double flowers that occur as mutants ('sports') in a group of single-flowered wild blossoms are often, but not always, sterile. Most wild plants set seed about a month after flowering. Collect seed when the capsule is dry and brown, an indication that the seeds are well ripened. Seed saved from soft, green, immature seed pods will have a very low germination rate, if indeed it germinates at all. In the case of berry-producing plants, collect only red ripe berries, not green ones. If you want to save seed from berries, it must be removed from the pulp and dried, but this step is not necessary if you intend to plant the berries soon.

Seeds retain their life force best when stored in a cool, dry place. Dry the seeds on paper for a week before putting them away, and remove any chaff that might have come with them. Be sure to label your collected seeds. I always include the source, either the name of the person who gave me the seeds or the place where I found them, when labeling mine.

A friend of ours once returned from a trip to Colorado with pockets full of wildflower seeds, Western columbine, lupine, Indian paintbrush, mariposa lily, and proceeded to scatter the seed in likely-looking pockets and patches around her property. The fact that she got few, if any, plants from those seeds is easily explained. Soil and climate in her Pennsylvania garden were quite different from that where the seeds originated. Several of the species collected were specific Western varieties not suited to Eastern soils and weather. And random scattering of seeds is chancy at best. Even under the most favorable natural conditions, few of the many seeds shed will survive. When going to the trouble of raising wildlings from seed, you might as well give yourself a good chance for success by establishing a nursery seedbed in the garden or planting the seeds in flats in a cold frame or even indoors under lights, where you can keep an eye on them. And finally, many wild seeds remain dormant until they've endured a spell of cold weather. Stratifying (exposing planted seeds to cold and even freezing temperatures) is a technique used by experienced gardeners to persuade dormant seeds to sprout. You can make it work for you too.

If you want to avoid the sort of disappointment my friend experienced, start your wildflower adventure by sowing seeds of plants that are likely to do well in your area, either wild plants you've seen growing nearby or certain flowers like the wild geranium, Jacob's ladder, columbine, and mayapple which seem to prosper under a wide variety of conditions. Later, when you've successfully raised some of the easy ones, you will be ready to experiment with some of the more rare and difficult wildflowers.

Growing wildflowers from seed is different from growing most garden vegetables. Many wildflowers are adapted to a rather narrow range of soil, sun, and moisture conditions, so that you are involved, really, in two adventures: (1) getting the seed to germinate and grow into a healthy seedling, which often takes longer for wildflowers than for vegetables; and (2) finding a plot or pocket of just the right soil in just the right place, where the plant will not only prosper but multiply. When working with plants that need very particular growing conditions, it is often a good idea to plant the seedlings in several likely places in hopes that one of them will prove to be satisfactory. Many of the plants described here are more adaptable than that, but the few that aren't are well worth trying, too.

Many wild plants appreciate a generous amount of humus in the soil, which you can provide by digging in compost or leaf mold. I would not apply heavy doses of fertilizer to wildlings, though. They would never have made it this far if they depended on such artificial boosts.

You can sow the seeds outdoors from fall through late winter to take advantage of the dormancy-breaking effect of freezing weather. Put the tray of planted seeds in your refrigerator or freezer for a week or so to duplicate these natural conditions when sowing seed at other times of year.

Flats of seedlings may be planted indoors in January or February, set outside to experience a month or so of cold weather, then brought inside to germinate under fluorescent plant lights. Flats planted in the fall may be wintered over in a cold frame. Or, if you don't use plant lights, but still prefer seed planting in flats to nursery-bed planting, you can leave those winter-planted flats outdoors in a protected spot, and transplant the seedlings when they germinate in spring. Stratifying, the practice of exposing planted seeds to a cold temperature, seems to be necessary for the germination of many wildflower seeds.

If you are planting the seeds directly in a garden bed or cold frame, prepare the soil first by digging in compost or leaf mold and, if your soil is heavy clay, a few shovelsful of sand. Rake the soil finely, press the seeds into it, and water lightly. Tiny seeds do not need to be covered but those measuring one-eighth inch or so should have a light sifting of fine soil pressed over them. Then scatter handfuls of straw or pine needles over the bed when the soil has frozen.

Or, you can sow the seed in flats filled with your favorite seed-starting mixture. I like equal parts of vermiculite, perlite, and finely milled sphagnum moss, moistened well before distributing the seeds. For varieties that don't take kindly to transplanting, use peat pots or individual clay pots or cut-down milk cartons.

Germination in wildflowers is far less uniform and usually much less prompt than in most garden flowers and vegetables. This is a protective mechanism that increases the probability that at least some plants will survive. It is not at all unusual to wait several months to see the first sprout, and some seeds will further confound you by waiting until next year to sprout. Keep the seedbed moist and shaded until some sign of life does appear, and then expose the seedlings to light as soon as they've germinated. One delightful aspect of raising wildflowers from seed is that the seedling plants often vary widely, giving you a choice of colors and sizes with which to work if you wish to continue saving and replanting seeds.

The following notes on the culture of individual wildflowers include some of the easiest to grow and most widely appreciated. They are the ones with which I am most familiar, but they are by no means the *only* wildflowers you can grow from seed. Consult specialized books and plant societies for more information. Although the trailing arbutus is one of the more difficult wildflowers to establish from seed, I've included it in the hope that some especially adventurous gardeners might find it possible to start new colonies of this delightfully fragrant spring-blooming wild plant. If you want to make the world a better place, you could do worse than to start by helping arbutus to make a comeback.

Arbutus, Trailing

Epigaea repens

My childhood memory of arbutus bouquets given to our family by friends is a haunting one. The heavy, sweet fragrance of the tubular pale-pink arbutus flowers, plus its habit of early spring bloom, are probably partly responsible for the plant's present rarity; people simply could not resist picking it. Unlike daisies, violets, and wild roses, arbutus doesn't grow back quickly. Whole plants, with their creeping prostrate growth pattern, were often uprooted by eager pickers. Few if any of those who gathered the plant realized how small a margin of survival it had – how difficult it is to transplant and how utterly dependent it is on highly specific soil fungi and bacteria in order to absorb the soil nourishment it needs. It is not only the fragrance that haunts me, but also the troubling thought that violence was done to a valued plant in the name of friendship. (And for less noble motives as well. It was once the custom to sell bunches of trailing arbutus in cities every spring, as holly and mistletoe are sold at Christmas.) I hope we are wiser now, but I wonder.

If you have near you the kind of acid, fairly poor, sandy or rocky soil near pines or hemlocks in which arbutus is known to survive, you might want to make a special effort to grow plants from seed. The small white five-lobed seed-containing berries ripen about the same time as wild strawberries, but they are often pilfered by squirrels and insects, even before they are ripe. Carefully bag the berries you hope to save. Or buy seed. Seeds this rare should be given watchful care – sown in a sterile seedling mix in the cold frame or grown under fluorescent lights for the first several months.

Keep the seedlings in the cold frame over their second winter, all the while guarding against drying out. Transplant them to several marked locations where you've dug in some soil scratched from around a mature trailing arbutus plant, if possible. Woods soil at the plant-root zone is often quite different in reaction and texture to that found on the surface, but do your best to get a sample without disturbing the established plant. For most of us, this step won't be possible. I know of only one living arbutus population and it is so fragile that I wouldn't think of disturbing it. Wildflower expert Edgar Wherry advises those who hope to grow arbutus to put the plants in soil that does not contain garden earthworms. Plant your seedlings where they will receive *some* sun, broken up by high trees. Plants grown in heavy shade won't bloom. The plants grow very slowly. If you are able to produce even one blooming plant in three to five years, consider yourself a mighty accomplished gardener. And then if you have even a single plant to call your own, you can gradually make increase from it by layering and sowing seed, both precarious projects with a rather high rate of failure, but worthwhile when you consider the possible alternative: extinct trailing arbutus. Mulch plants each winter with pine needles.

Black-eyed Susan
Rudbeckia hirta

A lovely flower to naturalize in meadows and by roadsides, this two-foot-tall biennial blooms in the summer of its second year. The much-beloved brown-centered yellow-petaled daisy form is often the start of a wildflower bouquet. It self-sows generously. To start plants where *you* want them, gather the seed when the seed head (the central cone) begins to fall apart and plant it in your nursery row immediately – no need to wait till winter. Move the plants to their intended place when they're several inches high.

Bloodroot
Sanguinaria canadensis

Easily started from seed and a strong self-sower, bloodroot makes a woodsy carpet of white-flowered bloom in early spring. The rounded, somewhat lobed leaves furl around the stem of the budding plant. Deciduous woods with neutral or moderately acid soil are an ideal habitat, providing the spring sun and summer shade that best suit the plant. Leaves usually disappear in summer. Fall-sown seeds generally germinate by spring. Since the plant is a perennial, it can form a large colony when it becomes established in a favorable spot. There is an open woods by the road, in a Midwestern state where we once lived, in which an impromptu dump has somehow started, the good green ground littered with bottles, cans, and old mattresses. Yet each year generous drifts of bloodroot bloom again there, like a blessing, between the cans. How long can they continue? Which force will prove stronger? Will the appealing beauty of the wildflowers somehow shame the litterers away? Or will the junk soon cover every open patch where once bloodroot had, at least in spring, the last word? Someday perhaps I will go back and see.

Blue-eyed Grass
Sysyrinchium angustifolium

These May- and June-blooming perennials reward the close observer with starry gold-centered true-blue blossoms dotting stiff, grassy, foot-high foliage. You'll find them in full sun in damp meadows, often overshadowed by taller weeds and grasses. Given a place of their own in the wild garden, they form a delightful perky bouquet and often self-sow freely. Collect the seeds in midsummer; once you have a colony of blue-eyed grass there will be a good supply of seedlings for transplanting.

Bunchberry
Cornus canadensis

These ground-hugging (four to eight inches high) relatives of the dogwood show their kinship in the finely tooled indented lines on their six leaves, and also the four-petaled 'flowers,' which are really bracts surrounding the tiny inconspicuous true flowers. In the Maine woods where I spent my childhood summers, bunchberry plants were still in bloom when we arrived from the city, dusty, full of expectation, hyperventilating the clean piney salt air. Later, when blueberries were ripe for picking, green bunchberries started to form, and by the time we packed to leave, at the end of the summer, the woods was jeweled with long-lasting clusters of red bunchberries. I often carried one last one as I stepped reluctantly into the loaded, homeward-bound car.

Bunchberries have rather specific requirements which are not easy to duplicate in the average backyard. In the humus-rich, highly acid soil (pH 4 to 4.5) and cool, damp, shady woods where they grow naturally, they spread by seed and rhizomes into large perennial colonies. In warmer climates, even with the proper pH, they'll produce fewer blooms and berries. Where summers are hot and shade is absent, effort would be better spent on other plants, but gardeners in New England, New York state, the north central United States, and Canada should find the bunchberry a worthwhile adventure. If you're trying to persuade bunchberries to grow outside their natural range, give them what the experts call a cool root run . . . place rocks over their root zones to keep them cool.

Butterfly Weed
Asclepias tuberosa

These showy orange-flowered perennials double your pleasure in their beauty by attracting butterflies. They are easy to grow from seed and do well in a sunny, well-drained spot. Poor drainage, especially in heavy soils, may cause winterkill. Sow seed in nursery beds in the fall, or indoors in flats in spring. Young seedlings transplant readily but mature plants are difficult to move successfully because they develop a long, thick taproot. Space the plants a good eighteen to twenty inches apart if you grow them in a flower border; they'll reach a height of two to three feet.

Cardinal Flower
Lobelia cardinalis

These stately perennials with their spectacular rich red flower spikes occur naturally at the edges of wet meadows and rocky stream beds, but they will flourish for several years in the perennial border, given a rich, moist, well-drained soil. A heaping shovelful of compost in the planting hole should help to provide these conditions. Cardinal flowers like moderately acid soil. They should be well mulched over winter because the roots remain close to the soil surface. Sow seeds from fall through winter in nursery beds or flats which you can bring indoors once they've been exposed to several good freezes. Transplant seedlings to their permanent location in late spring. If you have a stream on your place, I can't imagine a more effective way to enhance its beauty. The deep red tubular flowers are attractive to hummingbirds too.

Columbine
Aquilegia canadensis – red and yellow

Eastern Columbine

A. longissima (Southwest) – yellow, long

spurs, blooms later

A. coerulea (Rocky Mountains) – blue and white

The nodding, graceful red and yellow spurs of the wild columbine are borne on wiry stems rising above lobed gray-green rue-like leaves. They self-seed readily, often appearing in the most improbable rocky ledges. In fact, they seem to bloom most generously in a fairly lean soil; overly rich garden soil may just produce rank growth with few flowers. Very easy to grow from seed, wild columbines may even be started by scuffing seed into the soil right where you want them to grow, but you'll have more plants if you sow the seed, as soon as you gather or receive it, in flats or nursery beds and transplant the young seedlings to a fairly dry location with moderately acid soil and light shade. They'll bloom the second or third year. Older plants have a deep taproot, making them more difficult to transplant successfully.

Dutchman's-breeches
Dicentra cucullaria

Perky stalks of white upside-down breeches grow above finely-cut foliage on these ten-inch-high perennials. You'll find them in rich soil that is moderately acid, often on the Eastern slope of a hill. The foliage fades away in summer. Start the seed in fall or winter. Mature plants form a bulbous collection of tubers, which may be broken apart to start new plants.

Forget-me-not
Myosotis laxa

An ingratiating, low-growing, sprawling perennial, forget-me-nots are found wild in the muddy ground at the edges of streams. Their three-eighths-inch yellow-eyed sky blue flowers dot the upright stems that arise from the creeping rootstock. Our neighbors planted a border of them around a sunken bathtub pond they'd installed in their semi-shady backyard – a graceful way to camouflage the tub rim, and a perfect spot for the moisture-loving myosotis. Forget-me-nots self-sow readily. You can even scatter the seeds directly on moist soil where you want the plants to grow, but avoid sowing seed where stream banks are likely to overflow in early spring; although mature, well-rooted plants would be happy there, seeds would be washed away. Forget-me-nots also do well by the garden hose outlet, or in any other wet place where running or standing water is often present.

Gentian

Gentiana andrewsii – closed or bottle gentian

G. crinita – fringed gentian

Some years, when we let ourselves get too busy in late summer, the bottle gentians bloom unseen at the edge of our boggy meadow. No one should be that busy. These lovely deep-blue tubular flowers look like buds, but they never open. Happily, they are perennials, returning each year to bloom in the moist, humus-rich, mostly sunny places they love. The seeds are extremely fine, almost dust-like. Expose the planted seeds to freezing weather and expect spring germination from fall-planted seed. If you've brought flats indoors after subjecting them to frost, seedlings will appear sooner. The rare fringed gentian thrives under much the same conditions, but it is a biennial. Seeds ripen in October and should be planted right away. It is well worth your attention if you enjoy a good crusade, since it is not only a vanishing variety, but also quite beautiful.

Geranium

Geranium maculatum

One of the best to begin with, this pretty, agreeable perennial comes easily from seed and grows well in a wide variety of soils. The fifteen-inch-high plants bear lilac-pink open-faced flowers above at-tractive finely cut lobed leaves. Start seeds whenever you can obtain them, indoors or out. The plant self-seeds readily, too. Geranium is good with ferns in a semi-shady border.

Hepatica

Hepatica americana

H. acutiloba

One of our most welcome wild plants, hepatica is both early to bloom and lovely, with its delicate but colorful pink, white, or lav-ender-blue blossoms rising bravely above last year's three-lobed leaves. New leaves appear after blooming. Hepaticas like some dappled sun while in bloom with fairly consistent shade for the remainder of the growing season. Soil may be moderately acid to nearly neutral. (*Hepatica acutiloba,* which has pointed leaves, prefers neutral soil.) They do very well in our woods under oaks and maples. To be sure of catching the seeds, tie a small bag over the ripening seedpod. Plant the seeds as soon as you collect them, but don't expect to see much. Those that germinate in summer will form a small root but even the cotyledons (the first two seed leaves that precede the true leaves) don't appear until the following summer. Keep the seedlings shaded from direct sun and don't let them dry out. The roots are easily injured in moving, so rather than pick out individual plants, dig up a 'sod' or small clump of plants for transplanting to the wild garden or woods.

Jack-in-the-pulpit
Arisaema truphyllum

This childhood favorite is not hard to find in the seeding stage. Although the sheathed-spathe flower with its sounding-board pulpit may have collapsed by late summer, the red-berried central stalk remains. Rub off the flesh and plant the seeds as soon as you collect them, placing them one-half inch deep in a well-prepared seedbed. When planting seed in flats, you'll get quicker, more complete germination if you chill the planted flats for several weeks. Plant seedling 'jacks' in strongly acid soil well supplied with humus and not too dry. They're not really fussy plants, and even a single one, growing among ferns in that formerly wasted shady north side of your house, will soon become an old friend.

Jacob's Ladder
Polemonium reptans

Like the wild geranium, this is an adaptable plant that accepts different soil conditions and makes a pretty addition to a perennial border or spring bulb garden, where it forms a neat edging. The blue bell-like blossoms are borne in profusion above stems with many small, opposite leaflets which were evidently the inspiration for its common name. Altogether a very pretty, very easy plant, and one well worth growing. Start seeds indoors under lights or in the garden nursery bed. You'll find wild plants in open woods where soil is moderately acid to neutral. Full sun in early spring followed by partial shade in summer suits Jacob's ladder quite well.

Lupine
Lupinus perennis

The Eastern and Midwestern lupine grows about two feet tall, a foot shorter than its Western cousin. The pod-like flowers are purple, pink, or white, borne above leaves that are cut like palm fronds. Found in lean, sandy, acid soils, often near the coast, blooming-age lupines do not usually survive transplanting because they have a deep taproot. Young seedlings, moved before their roots have grown deep, should do well for you if you can approximate their ancestral growing conditions. Collect seed, which ripens in July, before it dries completely, and plant it right away. Wildflower expert Edgar Wherry suggests that seed be planted in soil dug from the base of the parent plant. It would no doubt be a good idea, as a matter of fact, to include some indigenous soil in the potting mixture for any wildflower seedling; often there are specific bacteria, fungi, or leaf molds which may be helpful in establishing the plant.

Mayapple
Podophyllum peltatum

An enthusiastic spreader when well established, the mayapple bears a single waxy white bloom under five- to eight-inch-wide umbrella-like leaves. The flower is followed, in late summer, by a yellow-green lemon-shaped edible fruit about the size of a wild plum. Animals eat the fruits, often before they are fully ripe, so you may need to cage or otherwise protect the one you have staked out for seeding stock. Remove the seeds from the pulp of the ripe fruit and stratify them as previously suggested. Set the plants in their permanent places while they are still small, before they develop the strong forked root that helps to ensure their survival from year to year. Mayapples like fairly moist, ordinary soil in open woods or pasture edges.

Shooting Star

Dodecatheon meadia – twelve inches high,

pink and white flowers

D. amethystinum – low, purple-pink blossoms

The shooting star is always a delightful find in the sort of moist, slightly-to-moderately acid, open woodsy slopes where it feels at home. Plants growing in heavy shade seldom bloom. Gather the seeds of these perennials when they ripen in July and stratify them. Later in the summer the foliage will disappear. Set out young plants in moist, humus-rich, well-drained soil.

Solomon's Seal

Polygonatum commutatum

This handsome leafy four-foot-tall perennial bears clusters of white tubular bell-like flowers drooping from the stem along its entire length. (False Solomon's seal is similar but has blossoms only on the tips of the stalk.) Not difficult to establish in the perennial border or woodland garden, Solomon's seal fares well in rich, somewhat acid soil with some shade. Gather the blue berries in fall, wash the pulp from the seeds, and plant them in a protected spot where they'll experience some winter freezing. When the plant is in bloom, look at it again. It's related to the lily of the valley. See?

Spring Beauty

Claytonia virginica

These delicate early-blooming perennials send you down on your knees for a closer look. The one-half-inch-diameter blooms, borne on thready stems amid grass-like foliage, are minutely striped in deep pink. Beautiful. At home in almost any moist, open woods with decent soil, they've been known to establish fine colonies in shady places in town when introduced. Watch the plant carefully, for it disappears after seeding. You might want to bag the seedpods to be sure of getting some. Spring beauty self-sows readily. When you're taking charge of the process, sow the ripe seed in the usual way and next year transplant the tiny first-year tubers to the place they're needed during the following summer. (They should bloom the third year.)

Trillium, Giant
Trillium grandiflorum

My Philadelphia neighbor ritually counted his trillium blooms each spring. One year he had forty of them in his front yard. The rose-colored blossoms that followed the white ones on these showy perennials were, I soon learned, just the later stage of the fading flower and not a new flowering. Wild trilliums are found in moist, humus-rich woods, often among mixed evergreens and deciduous trees. Unlike other trilliums, especially the difficult acid-loving painted trillium, the great trillium thrives in near-neutral soil and accepts ordinary garden soil, given a good supply of humus and some summer shade. Extract the seeds from the fruits and wash off the pulp. Stratify the seed as suggested earlier and transplant the small resulting bulblets into soil improved with compost or leaf mold. Great trillium plants grown from seed sometimes take as long as five to ten years to bloom.

Trout Lily
Erythronium americanum

The trout lily, or dogtooth violet as some would have it, has mystified me for quite some time. Why are there so many plants that don't bloom? How can I get the ones I transplant to bloom? Trout lilies are difficult to move, for their bulbs often lie too deep for easy digging in rocky or root-filled soil. If you can get seeds, you can be more certain that the plants will survive transplanting when moved as seedlings. According to former Wildflower Society president P. L. Ricker, writing in the 1961 USDA Yearbook *Seeds*, trout lily plants don't bloom until the seventh year; all that time the bulb is growing progressively deeper. This partly explains the many non-blooming plants usually seen in large colonies of these perennials; some are no doubt too young to bloom. Crowding or lack of sun can also retard blooming. The trout lily is a lovely find in damp, rich woods or near streams. Its yellow, lily-shaped flower with curved-back petals rises on a five- to eight-inch stem over mottled oval leaves. The plant often dies back after its April/May blooming season. Sometimes seeds are difficult to find. They should ripen in June, and may be sown in fall for germination the following spring. The most important point to remember in transplanting young trout lily plants, other than the necessity for duplicating their original conditions as much as possible, is to plant the little bulbs at least three inches deep. A soil range from neutral to highly acid seems to be acceptable.

Virginia Bluebells

Mertensia virginica

A patch of these fifteen- to twenty-four-inch perennials with their clusters of clear sky blue bell-shaped flowers is a treat for the eye in late April and May. They are found naturally in damp, partly shady spots, often at the edges of streams that overflow with spring snow melt. I've grown Virginia bluebells in moist humus-rich soil in a small wildflower strip on the north side of a suburban garage, far from any stream, and they bloomed beautifully each year. Virginia bluebells are easy to raise from seed. They self-sow freely and the seed should be easy to obtain if you can find a colony of *Mertensia.* Where conditions are ideal for this flower, it may often be found in great profusion. Sow the seeds in February, indoors or out, and give the seedlings rich, not too acid soil in a damp place with part shade. Like many other wildflowers, Virginia bluebells die back in the summer after they've bloomed. Mark their spot if you're afraid you might accidentally dig them up then (as I've been known to do). If you also grow borage, you'll notice that the related Virginia bluebells also have the large long oval leaves, pinkish buds, and perfectly blue flowers that typify the borage family, to which it belongs.

A publisher once asked me to write a book on how to get free plants from the wild. The thrust of what he had in mind, though, was weighted more toward getting something for nothing than toward conservation and propagation of some of these wild treasures for their own sakes, and I could not, in all conscience, agree to do the book. It is all too easy to dig up wildflowers, and all too difficult to do them justice when you get them home. Growing wildlings from seed, though, prevents much thoughtless uprooting and actually results in an increase in the number of thriving wild plants. It is, in fact, a lifetime adventure in which both the casual gardener and the passionate gardener can find challenge and satisfaction.

Grow Your Own Teas

Bee Balm

There are probably dozens of good herb teas that you can grow or forage, and others available commercially as blends. The teas I'm about to describe are those that we've actually grown or foraged ourselves. Far from being an exhaustive list of all the good teas that can be found, this is just a summary of the beginning we've made.

Herb teas taste good. They are an inclusive beverage; children can drink them along with their parents. When I make herb tea, we all drink tea, and that's good too. Most of the herb teas we make cost us nothing, other than in some cases the initial investment in plants or seeds. We have a wide choice of flavors to suit our individual tastes and the whim of the moment.

Bee Balm

Monarda fistulosa

M. didyma

Bee Balm, also called Oswego tea, or bergamot, makes a pungent, refreshing tea. The red-flowered form, *Monarda didyma,* has a finer flavor than the coarser lavender-flowered wild form, *Monarda fistulosa.* These three-foot-tall, rather bushy perennial plants prefer moist soil and thrive in either full sun or light shade. You can start with a division begged from a friend or purchased from a nursery, or plant seed indoors or in a special nursery row outdoors in April. Plants should be spaced eighteen inches apart.

Chamomile

Matricaria chamomilla

Anthemis nobilis

All chamomiles are aromatic. Both the bushy, foot-tall annual plants (*Matricaria chamomilla*) and the sprawling perennial (*Anthemis nobilis*) flourish in fairly rich soil, preferring clay to sand. Perennial plants from late summer seeding will flower the following spring. The annual form will bloom in eight weeks from seed. The feathery seedlings are delicate and easily lost in the crush of weeds. Keep them well weeded and mulched and space them almost one foot apart. It is easier to control the weeds if you grow the herb in a row rather than a solid bed.

I often start the plants indoors in March, sowing the fine seeds in flats and transplanting the seedlings to stand three inches apart in a larger flat. Light seems to promote germination of the seeds. Although the seeds tend to lose a good bit of viability after a year, I've still gotten a nice stand of plants from a packet of two-year-old seed.

The daisy-like blossom of the plant, with its yellow cone-shaped center surrounded by short white petals, is the part used for tea. Picking the blossoms requires some patience, but it can be a restful task if you just sit next to the plants with your picking basket and snap off the plump little daisies with your thumb.

Since reading that chamomile tea helps to relieve allergic reactions due to hay fever and other sensitivities, we have been giving it our serious attention. The results aren't in yet, but we're enjoying the tea. The idea is to drink the tea daily for a month or two before the time of onset of a seasonal allergy like hay fever.

Comfrey

Symphytum

Comfrey steeped alone comes on a little too righteous for our taste. When we brew it with mint, though, we get the double value of the comfrey nutrients and the mint flavor. We drink it often.

Comfrey is easy to start and hard to discourage. Plant root cuttings three to four inches deep and three feet apart. Don't put them in the vegetable garden, though, because they will keep coming back faithfully every year, thanks to that deep root. Comfrey is good enough to deserve a patch in its own right, or at least its own corner by a shed. We keep our patch well mulched with hay and take about five cuttings a season.

Comfrey leaves for drying should be picked before the plant flowers for optimum food value. We dry ours on screens in the attic in the hottest days of midsummer, since the large leaf takes more time to dry than the smaller mint leaf.

If one of the children has gashed a leg in a fall from a bike or my husband has cut his hand while working in the woods, I try to see that they get a few extra doses of comfrey-mint tea and also use an infusion of the comfrey leaves to soak the cut in order to promote healing. Another good trick with comfrey is to pot up a root or rooted cutting to grow in the house. It makes a fine, attractive houseplant from which you can pluck leaves all winter for freshly brewed tea. Comfrey is a good source of calcium, phosphorus, potassium, vitamins A and C, and trace minerals. A good tea to have on your side all year round.

Elderberry

Sambucus

Elderberry tea, sweetened with honey, tastes like a hot fruit punch. The unsweetened brew is dark and rich enough to substitute for coffee. We make elderberry tea from the dried berries. As Euell Gibbons related in his book *Stalking The Wild Asparagus,* drying somehow removes the rather rank taste that fresh elderberries have.

I think it's a safe guess that most wild elderberries in our country are eaten by the birds. There's no reason, though, why the rest of us shouldn't get in on the harvest. Early summer is a good time to spot wild elderberry bushes, when the creamy flat umbels of flowers, a bit like palm-sized Queen Anne's lace, are in bloom. Elderberry pickers seldom snitch a taste of their bounty as they pick. The raw berries are not what you'd call delicious. But cooked and sweetened, or dried and brewed as tea, they are as rich and good in flavor as they are in nourishment. One pound of elderberries, according to the *USDA Handbook of the Nutritional Contents of Foods,* contains: 2560 IU vitamin A, 154 mg. vitamin C, 0.30 mg. thiamin, 0.27 mg. riboflavin, 2.3 mg. niacin.

You can forage for wild elderberries, you can transplant wild bushes into damp places on your own property, and you can raise cultivated elderberries. Adams and Johns are two of the reliable named varieties. The cultivated berry is larger than the wild one, but it has less flavor.

We have had wonderful crops of large, juicy cultivated elderberries from a bush planted in a partially shaded, damp corner where rainy runoff from the goat pen kept it well fertilized. Here on our farm, we have a good patch of wild elderberries growing at the edge of our swamp. It is so far off the beaten path, though, a regular bird sanctuary, that you can guess what happens to most of the berries. We've never been able to get there in time to pick any ripe ones. So we are gradually transplanting young bushes to the rim of a damp ditch not far from the barn, where we can keep an eye on the berries and harvest them as soon as they're ready. We've planted our cultivated bushes there, too.

Look for the wild elderberry in damp, rich land – along culverts, bordering swamps, next to rivers, by railroad tracks. The berries are ready to pick by late August in our area. Let them ripen on the bush as completely as possible, but keep an eye on them. When they're really ripe, the birds often strip them overnight. In picking, we break off the whole cluster of berries on its stem. We leave them on the stem until they're dry, so that they are more completely exposed to the air.

Elderberry bushes don't mind a little shade. When they are happy where they are, in a moist spot with generous applications of fertilizer, they can grow very fast.

Lemon Verbena
Lippia citriodora

Lemon Verbena really does have a marvelous aroma of lemons. It makes a delicious brew either by itself or mixed with another less interesting tea.

The plant is a perennial in its native Chile. It thrives in well-drained, reasonably fertile, fairly light soil, not too acid. Since it is frost-tender, we bring our lemon verbena inside to winter on the sunny kitchen windowsill. The plant often responds to a change in scenery by dropping all its leaves. Don't let that worry you. Just keep talking to it, water it weekly and give it plenty of light, and you should find that new green shoots will appear within several weeks.

Just brushing a leaf with your fingers will release some of that clean refreshing lemon fragrance. If you have more verbena than you need for tea, you may want to use some to make potpourri, a blend of dried spices, rose petals, and aromatic herbs.

I know of no source for seeds of this plant, but rooted plants may be ordered by mail from herb dealers, if you can't find them locally. To start new plants from cuttings, be sure to use only tender new growth, not the woody older stems that have already hardened and are not likely to root. Verbena cuttings, in my experience, root somewhat less readily than those of mint, but from three or four cuttings, I count on getting at least one good plant.

Linden

Tilia; T. cordata; T. europaea;
T. platyphyllos

Linden tea is a haunting, perfumy beverage that most people enjoy at first sip. The linden tree bears clusters of pale, waxy flowers in late June and early July here in south central Pennsylvania. The flowers contain vitamin C and carotene. The fragrance of the blossoms on a wild linden tree growing on the edge of our woods perfumes the air for a week in July.

Gather the blossoms on a clear dry day. Some connoisseurs prefer just-opened buds rather than full-blown, but tea made from fully opened flowers is still delicious. The tree will most likely be humming with bees. Brew up a pot of the fresh tea and dry the remaining blossoms in a hot, dry, dark place. We have picked enough blossoms from the low branches of one big old capacious linden to supply us for the year.

I've seen blossoming linden trees on city streets and in city parks. Two gorgeous old lindens flank the approach to Jefferson's Monticello. Once you've encountered the linden in bloom, you'll know it from a good distance the next time. The tree grows wild by the roadside in some Eastern and Midwestern states.

In Europe, especially in France, the gathering of linden blossoms for 'tisane' is a ritual carried out yearly with the kind of overtones that only long dependence on the land can impart.

The linden tree is a fine ornamental, well worth planting as a lawn or shade tree. If you want to plant your own linden, order the European or small-leafed variety, a more consistent bloomer (*T. cordata* or *T. europaea* rather than *T. americana*). Give it a spot with good moist but well-drained soil and mulch it well during the early years. It will take a few years to get those first blossoms, but they'll be worth the wait!

Mint

Mentha

M. citrata – orange mint

M. spicata – spearmint

M. piperita – peppermint

M. rotundifolia – apple mint

Mint, that old dooryard favorite, grows almost everywhere in one or another of its many forms. You're most likely to have apple mint, with its woolly, rounded leaves; or spearmint, with its pointed, almost hairless leaves; or peppermint, with its pungent peppermint aroma.

A square stem is the characteristic sign of the aromatic mint family. Most mints thrive in moist places. Light shade helps them to do well in drier locations. Plant rooted slips or portions of a divided mint clump about a foot apart. Mint seems easy to grow and sometimes spreads persistently, but if you take it too much for granted, weeds will crowd it out and you'll have to begin again. While mints as a class accept a variety of soil conditions, they will die out if given a heavy dose of wood ashes. Having assumed that mints were practically indestructible, I was puzzled when the thick clump of apple mint by our back doorstep petered out. Enlightenment came when I read, in Audrey Wynne Hatfield's book *How to Enjoy Your Weeds,* that 'mint is badly affected by bonfire ash.' And that is just what I had given it, in a misguided burst of generosity. It's taken several seasons, the transplanting of the bed, and begging new starts from friends, to build up my mint patch again.

We also like orange mint, an easy-rooting, rather sprawling plant with mostly hairless leaves and a delightful orangy aroma. It makes an excellent, full-flavored tea either fresh or dried. Mint has the virtue of blending well with other teas and giving flavor to leafy brews like comfrey that don't have much flavor of their own.

Rose

Rosa; R. rugosa; R. multiflora

Rose hip tea is winter vitamin insurance. The vitamin C-rich hips may be dried on screens for use as a nourishing cold weather tea. We keep reading that rose hips taste like apples. As far as we are concerned, plain rose hip tea doesn't have an awful lot of flavor, but it is mild and blends well with a richer flavored tea like mint or elderberry.

Look for rose hips — the red, ripe seedpod of the rosebush — in your flower garden, on your hedgerow, or in the wild. Hips of any rose are good to use for tea, as long as the plant has not been subjected to noxious sprays. You're more likely to find an abundance of hips on bushes of single-flowered roses, which are easier for the bees to pollinate than the more complex double blossom. Vitamin C content varies somewhat with variety, but all are worth using.

If you want to plant roses especially for the harvest of hips, choose the *Rosa rugosa*, a hardy bush with somewhat wrinkled leaves and single white or rose flowers. Plant the bush on well-drained land where it will receive full sun. You can increase your *rugosa* plantings by dividing a well-established clump or planting seeds from the hips. The *rugosa* also spreads by underground stolons. Since it is a distinct species, the seeds will come true to the parent plant. (Crossing can occur only within a species.) The most gorgeous hips we've ever seen were those of a *Rosa rugosa* growing by the road in the Pocono Mountains of Pennsylvania. The hips were as big as large grapes. We even marked the spot on our map.

Some old farms have hedge plantings of *Rosa multiflora*. These have smaller hips, but when they are plentiful you can gather many in a short time. If you want to can rose hip extract, add lemon juice or vinegar to the infusion because rose hips are low in acid. Freezing the extract in cubes is a good way to make it easily available for use in teas and soups. But drying is easiest of all.

Tea Blends

When you've mastered the growing and preparation of several herb teas, you might like to try your hand at blending your own tea mixtures. Start small, with a pinch of this and a whiff of that, and when you hit on a tasty combination, write down the ingredients immediately. Here is a list of some edible plants, both wild and cultivated, from which you can choose in concocting your tea blends.

ROOTS
Comfrey
Ginseng
Sweet Birch
 (inner bark)

FLOWERS
Chamomile
Feverfew
Hibiscus
Linden
Red Clover

FRUIT
Elderberries
Rose Hips

SEEDS
Anise
Caraway
Fennel

LEAVES
Basil
Blackberry
Blueberry
Comfrey
Lemon Balm
Lemon Grass
Lemon Verbena
Marjoram
Mints

Mullein
New Jersey Tea
 (*Ceanothus
  americanus*)
Parsley
Pennyroyal
Raspberry
Rosemary
Sage
Strawberry
Sweet Goldenrod
 (*Solidago
  odora*)
Thyme
Wintergreen

Tea Tips

HINTS FOR PICKING AND DRYING HERB TEAS

1. Pick the leaves or flowers when fully developed and before they fade.
2. Choose a dry, sunny day to harvest your tea materials.
3. After picking, sun robs herbs of flavor and color. Keep drying leaves in a dark, hot place with good air circulation.
4. Thin-stemmed herbs in small amounts may be tied in small bunches and hung from nails on attic rafters.
5. Berries, large quantities of leaves, and fleshy-stemmed leaves like comfrey dry best when spread out on a large, flat surface. We use old window screens covered with clean paper or old sheets. We have also used large pieces of corrugated cardboard cut from commercial movers' cartons as bases for drying unstripped elderberries and even comfrey.
6. When the leaves have dried enough to crumble when rubbed between the fingers, or the berries are hard and shriveled and resist thumbnail denting, the tea is ready to package. Press it lightly into jars or cans and seal it well.
7. Store herbs in a cool, dry spot.

HINTS FOR BREWING HERB TEAS

1. Dried tea is more potent, volume for volume, than fresh.
2. For most leafy teas, one tablespoon of the dried crumbled leaves to a cup of boiling water is a good proportion. One to two teaspoons of dried elderberries to a cup is about right.
3. Rather than boil the leaves in water, the method preferred for retaining vitamins and volatile oils is to pour boiling water over the tea, allow it to steep for five to ten minutes, and then reheat gently. We like to keep a pot of herb tea brewing on top of our wood box stove in the kitchen.
4. An enamel or china teapot makes a better flavored tea than a metal one.
5. Coarse leaves like comfrey may be steeped directly in the pot. We use a tea ball for finer teas. Woven grass tea strainers, available in many kitchen specialty shops, may be used when pouring the tea into the cups, to filter out stray leaves and flowers.
6. Mild flavored teas like rose hip or comfrey may be perked up with lemon and sweetened with honey.
7. For iced tea, make a double-strength infusion of your favorites.

A Traditional Medicinal Garden

Pennyroyal

Most people probably think of intricate knot gardens with elaborate geometric beds when they hear the term 'colonial garden.' It is true that many early gardens were constructed on this formal, mannered order, especially on large estates, elegant town properties, and in homes where there were plenty of servants to take care of the weeding and clipping. Knot gardens require meticulous planning and intensive continuous care to keep them shapely and prevent weed take-over.

The average early American garden was less formal and more useful. It was, in fact, an indispensable resource from which the colonial housewife plucked not only fresh 'sallets' and 'garden sass' (a more recent old New England term for vegetables) but also, and often more crucially important, the herbs she depended on to keep her family well and cure their ills. Indeed, so vital was the eighteenth-century kitchen garden that even in a household with many children or abundant hired help, the woman of the house reserved to herself the responsibility of growing and preparing simples, as the early herbal remedies were called.

The form of these early gardens grew out of the circumstances of the times. In settlements where Indian raids were a regular threat, families built their houses close together in little towns, with the large open fields for raising crops situated just at the edge of town. Beside each house there was room for a small garden, which was often enclosed, along with the house, in a tall stockade fence. Later, in more gracious and less precarious times, and especially in the South, low dense hedges of boxwood were used to outline and to partly protect the kitchen garden.

In such a circumscribed plot, every inch counts. For that reason, even the informal herb gardens had a sense of order, an 'each plant in its place' layout, that permitted the raising of a maximum number of plants in a minimal space. Paths often crossed the garden, but in the smallest gardens the beds between paths were usually planted in a solid block of vegetables or herbs, rather than in space-wasting rows. The effect is one of casual but disciplined abundance.

Eighteenth-century family kitchen gardens were largely green gardens. By the early nineteenth century the wholesale raising of ornamental flowers in the style of the colorful, jumbled English cottage garden became commonplace, gradually replacing the herbs on which earlier generations had depended.

More than one hundred different plants were widely grown in these early gardens, and most of them served a purpose. Even the flowering plants – gilly flowers, marigolds, calendulas, flax, hollyhocks, bouncing bet – were grown for healing, eating, or household use. A great many gardens also harbored one or two varieties of poisonous plants, which were sometimes used in small doses to dull pain or induce sleep. In addition, according to the doctrine of signatures, still taken seriously during the eighteenth century, plant shapes and colors were considered clues to their efficacy in treating certain diseases. Thus the plant hepatica, with its liver-shaped leaf, was thought to be an effective treatment for hepatic ailments. We may smile at this unsophisticated reasoning, but as Ann Leighton suggests in *Early American Gardens,* it was not an illogical outgrowth, at the time, of the Puritan's conviction that the earth was created for man's use. What could be more natural than to suppose that the Creator had somehow marked the plants to help man discover their proper uses?

The books of the seventeenth-century herbalists, John Gerard, John Parkinson, and Nicholas Culpeper, were noted for their copious use of secondhand information, as well as for their helpful descriptions of plants and their common uses. These herbalists influenced the shaping of early gardens. One of their books – Gerard's *Herball,* Culpeper's *English Physician and Complete Herbal,* or Parkinson's *Paradisi in Sole Paradisus Terrestris* – was often kept on the mantel next to the Bible in colonial homes. Eating periwinkle (*Vinca minor*), for example, was said to 'cause love between man and wife.' Other prescriptions, such as eating wild cress or watercress for scurvy, and consuming sorrel when citrus fruits were scarce, were right as rain. Both of these green leafy foods, and many others similarly recommended, contain significant amounts of vitamin C, the official antiscorbutic. On the whole, despite some of the bizarre cures that make me, for one, very glad to be living here and now, I find it remarkable that so many plants now recognized for their high vitamin and mineral content were recommended and used correctly by the traditional herbalists, with only hearsay, tradition, and observation to guide them.

After a century of concentration on flowers and other ornamentals, American gardeners once again plant more vegetable than flowers, a trend which has become increasingly evident in the 1970s. We have come full circle – back to relying on useful plants. Perhaps it is appropriate then for the twentieth-century gardener to turn to these early gardens for helpful lore. Certainly it is true that the combination of useful plants, grown in a compact space, close by the kitchen door, is a hard one to beat.

Whether you call it an herb garden, a kitchen garden, a seasoning, medicinal, or knot garden, you may find great satisfaction in setting up a green and ferny corner alive with small neat mounds of thyme, tall lacy heads of dill, shrubby needle-leaved rosemary, tall imposing boneset, mat-like satiny wild ginger, vigorous vining hops, fragrant varieties of geranium. A welcoming garden for your guests, who will delight in plucking an aromatic leaf as they enter or leave your home. A source of savory seasonings, insect-repellent aromatics, and even helpful healing tonics, such a small kitchen garden will give you pleasure out of all proportion to its size. One of my gardening friends who is also an accomplished cook has a three- by five-foot semicircle near the back (main) door of her eighteenth-century stone house planted to herbs and pansies. There's sage, dill, thyme, geraniums, parsley, chives – just a few of each. That little plot seems to attract even more admiring attention than the brightly colored flowers planted in conventional style in borders surrounding the house.

Craftspeople with a feeling for the old subtle colors may want to grow dye plants like tansy, juniper, coreopsis, and rue (for the root). Or, if herbal healing interests you, experiment with some of the mild nontoxic healing agents like chamomile, garlic, fennel, catnip, horehound, and sage. Group them in a small plot, add an edging of parsley or chives, and you've revived an old and ever-useful tradition, the kitchen garden.

Here is a representative sampling of plants found in early gardens, with notes on growing and using them. I've left out the dangerously poisonous ones and those chosen for the significance of their shapes, and have included only some of those herbs and flowers which are worth growing today for use or ornament. Admittedly a partial listing, this includes the plants that seemed to me most useful.

Basil

Ocimum basilicum

Many present day gardeners grow basil especially to season their tomatoes. It was a favorite Old World and colonial herb, though, long before tomatoes were accepted as edible. The dark opal variety, with its deep purple leaves, makes an attractive pot plant but a somewhat murky addition to cooked greens. Plant basil seed or pre-started plants about the same time you set out your tomato plants. It likes warm weather and full sun. Allow a foot between plants, which will grow to a height of one and one-half to two feet. Some herbalists brew basil tea to remedy headache and nervous tension.

Calendula

Calendula officinalis

Also called pot marigold, calendula is a self-sowing annual bearing orange or yellow flowers, used in soups, broths, and also, in the seventeenth and eighteenth centuries, powdered and mixed with lard, turpentine, and resin to make a salve, and preserved in syrup and jam. Even today calendula is recommended by some herbalists for healing skin problems such as warts and ulcers. (See page 58 for more complete growing directions.)

Catnip

Nepeta cataria

A rather strong, gray-green-leaved, rank-growing mint. Not the best choice for tea if you have the more mellow apple mint, woolly mint, or spearmint in your garden, but a well-known traditional tea plant, especially esteemed for its soothing effect on the digestive system. It is also a good insect chaser. Strew a few sprigs on your kitchen shelves and counters to banish ants. The effect lasts three to four days and then the cuttings must be renewed. Catnip needs full sun but tolerates poor soil.

Chamomile

Matricaria chamomilla – annual

Anthemis nobilis – perennial

A low-growing ferny-leaved plant bearing small cone-shaped daisy-like blossoms which are steeped to make tea. Often taken to soothe the stomach and calm the nerves, chamomile tea is a sweet aromatic brew that is usually enjoyed with the first sip. (See page 99 for growing notes.) A gardening friend in New Zealand writes about planting a small chamomile lawn. Can you imagine anything more delightful?

Chervil
Anthriscus cerefolium

A lacy-leafed annual that unlike most herbs prefers part shade. Sow seed in a well-drained spot. The plants, which grow to eighteen inches tall, grow best in cool weather. The mild anise flavor makes chervil a good addition to the salad bowl, as indeed it has been for hundreds of years. When using chervil in cooked dishes, add it just before serving; heat destroys its aromatic oils.

Clove Gillyflower
Dianthus caryophyllus

The spicy scented pink of our present rock gardens and perennial beds was once prepared in syrup to remedy fever, heart trouble, and plague. Ann Leighton, in her excellent book *Early American Gardens*, explains that the term 'gillyflower,' which was also used to describe stocks and wallflowers, indicates that the plant blooms in July. Pinks need good well-drained soil and full sun. White, pink, and red varieties are available. The plant is a perennial and may be started from seed or propagated by division, layering, or rooting cuttings. No pinks have ever smelled so spicy to me as those in the New England garden of my childhood. A few clumps of pinks punctuating the kitchen garden make the quick assembly of a fragrant nosegay an easy pleasure. Such a tussie-mussie, as these small floral offerings were called, may be made almost entirely of green herbs with a few bright floral accents.

Comfrey
Symphytum officinale

A strong-growing perennial herb that should be cut before flowering to steep in tea or cook as a green vegetable. (See page 100.) The old herbalists, according to garden historian Ann Leighton, averred that the flesh of cut meat cooked with comfrey would rejoin. It *is* a fact, however, that comfrey, especially the stems, contains allantoin, a healing agent of proven effectiveness. Anyway, comfrey is good in soups, salads, and tea. Give it full sun and three feet of space on each side.

Corn Salad
Valerianella olitoria

Also called lamb's-lettuce, corn salad, along with lettuce, endive, rocket, carrots, and radishes, was an esteemed 'sallet' plant in early American times and earlier. These 'sallets,' incidentally, were often cooked and usually included a mixture of no less than four, and usually more, herbs.

Elecampane
Inula helenium

A robust, hairy-leaved perennial growing two to four feet high, elecampane bears large bright yellow daisy-like flowers. Recommended for a wide variety of ills, from what Galen called 'passions of the hucklebones' (sciatica) to cough, itching, worms, shortness of breath, and digestive problems, elecampane dominated the traditional garden in utility as well as in size. Only the root was used. It is grown by herbal healers even today for its effect on respiratory problems.

Fennel
Foeniculum vulgare dulce

An aromatic, anise-flavored annual plant that closely resembles dill, fennel was used, among other things, to encourage milk flow in the nursing woman and to treat kidney ailments. Present-day uses, apart from its excellence in salads and as a cooked vegetable, include brewing leaves and stems for a hot facial and using fennel solution as an eyewash. All parts of the plant, seed, root, stalk, and leaf, are edible and good. Start seed in early spring. Fennel is sometimes planted in a bed of its own because it seems to inhibit growth of several other garden vegetables including beans and tomatoes. (See *Vegetables Money Can't Buy* for more growing information.)

Feverfew
Chrysanthemum parthenium

This old healing staple, used to heal inflammation, depression, and toothache, earns a place in today's garden by virtue of its neat habit of growth and attractive white and yellow button-like flowers with small daisy-style petals. Whenever I've grown a garden, I've cherished feverfew for bouquets. The plant is perennial and self-sows freely.

Flax
Linum usitatissimum

Flax was grown in the fields for fiber to make cloth, but even more often in the garden for seed. The pulverized seeds were used in salves and poultices to reduce inflammation and swelling. When I was in nursing school in the early fifties we learned to make flaxseed poultices as a routine healing measure for patients recovering from thyroid surgery (one of the specialties of the Lahey Clinic at that time). (See page 73 for growing notes.)

Hops
Humulus lupulus

Colonists brought hops seed with them from England and gathered the flowers for use in making beer and yeast. Pioneer women, unaware that the native American hops grew wild in many parts of the West and Midwest, made sure to tuck a packet of hops seed in their wagons when they set out on their westward journeys. Hops vines thrive on well-drained soil in areas that receive regular rain; they don't do well in excessively dry places. According to vegetable expert Victor Tiedjens, the flavor imparted by hops varies with the soil on which it is grown. Tiedjens also warns that poor air circulation can lead to mildew problems. When it gets a good foothold, though, this exuberant perennial vine will cover a fence, trellis, or stone wall. Seed is next to impossible to germinate in hot weather unless you refrigerate it for six weeks before planting. Plant root cuttings or seedlings two feet apart. You might also try fall planting. There are male and female hops plants. The female blossoms are used to make beer. Gertrude Harris, in her book *Foods of the Frontier*, writes that blossoms with the pollen on them make the best yeast. Early Americans picked the young shoots for salads. The drooping, papery, compound blossoms make pleasantly softening additions to stiff arrangements of dried plants.

Horehound
Marrubium vulgare

Anyone who has ever sampled the musky, aromatic, sweet/bitter flavor of horehound cough drops can appreciate that this penetrating herb was a popular remedy for all kinds of coughs, colds, and throat ailments. In many places, it still is, as a tea, a syrup made from the sweetened tea, or as lozenges made by cooking the syrup to the hard-crack stage. Early herbalists also recommended horehound for liver, spleen, consumption, and childbirth. Plant rooted cuttings of this hardy perennial a foot apart in a sunny place where it will receive plenty of moisture while enjoying good drainage. An ancient plant, horehound is one of the five bitter herbs traditionally eaten at the Passover Feast.

Houseleek
Sempervivum tectorum

Also called 'hens and chickens,' the houseleek is a common dooryard plant that no one, it seems, ever plants; it is just there. Frequently to be found around the foundations and back steps of old houses, houseleeks make good perennial edging and rock-garden plants. Their ancient uses were mainly external applications for the healing of burns, ulcers, skin inflammations, corn removal, and gout. Some of the seventeenth century (and earlier) herbalists maintained that a planting of houseleeks could fend off lightning. Although no one expects that of it any more, it is still used, especially in Europe, to heal skin problems and relieve insect stings. Medicine or not, it is an attractive, long-lasting, trouble-free plant to have around.

Lavender
Lavandula officinalis

The New England colonists soon learned that the rooted slips of lavender they brought with them would not flourish in the north unless given a sheltered spot close to a building or hedge. Winterkill and poor soil drainage are the worst enemies of lavender. I've lost plants that were unprotected from west wind and on soggy soil. Lavender has few if any insect pests; in fact it has the property of repelling moths and ticks, and probably other insects as well. Gravelly soil well supplied with limestone will make lavender feel at home. Although the plant is a perennial, count on replacing it every few years if you live north of Maryland. Just keep young plants coming from rooted cuttings or root divisions. Lavender grows very slowly from seed. The plant forms an attractive bushy mound of aromatic gray-green leaves. Cut the leafy sprigs just before the buds open and dry in a warm, dark place. Dried lavender sachets stored with clothing help to repel insects and smell perfectly delightful when you open the linen closet door.

Lemon Balm
Melissa officinalis

An all-purpose lemony-flavored aromatic mint relative recommended in traditional herbal practice for healing of heart palpitations, nervous disorders, fever, and depression. A salve was made of the leaves, which were also often tossed into bath water for their refreshing effect. The blossoms attract bees, but to make tea the stems should be cut before the plant blossoms. Try snipping leaves into salads, too. Lemon balm is a perennial, growing about eighteen inches tall. It self-sows readily and may be started from seed, cuttings, or root division. Ordinary soil will be fine, and even part shade, if you are short of sunny space. The thick, bushy plant is a good one to plant by the door for plucking leaves to sniff as you go about your errands.

Marjoram

Majorana hortensis

formerly *Origanum majorana* – sweet

Origanum vulgare – wild

One of the most ancient of herbs, marjoram was a widely accepted remedy for asthma, rheumatism, and what the herbalist Gerard so expressively called 'wamblings of the stomacke.' In Elizabethan times it was a favorite strewing herb. Bertha Reppert, who grows and sells herbs in her Mechanicsburg, Pennsylvania, Rosemary Shop, suggests making a small pillow of dried marjoram for asthma sufferers. It is a delightful component of nosegays and herb wreaths, too, not to mention its excellence in cooking, to flavor soups, stews, omelets, sausage, and salads. Sweet marjoram has a more delicate flavor than oregano, the wild form.

Marjoram adds texture and shape to the dooryard garden. The attractive plant grows eight to twelve inches high, with many small branches bearing small gray-green oval leaves and round, knot-like flower buds. It prefers soil that is not overly acid and like most herbs does well in a sunny, well-drained spot. Many practitioners of the art of companion planting feel that marjoram improves both flavor and growth of its neighboring plants. To start from seeds, plant the tiny seeds in flats indoors and set them out after frost. You can also seed them right in the row if you've raked the soil fine. A half-hardy perennial, marjoram seldom lives over the winter for me but will survive in the South if given some protection.

Parsley

Petroselinum hortense

A perfect edging plant, parsley forms a low neat row of intensely green fine-cut perky leaves. Gardeners of other centuries grew it for flavoring soups and garnishing meats just as we do, and they also used the seed for medicinal purposes. Parsley is a biennial, producing seed the second year. It does well in heavy soil, doesn't mind acid soil, and will even thrive in part shade, although it produces more heavily in full sun. It is occasionally visited by a yellow, black, and green striped caterpillar – the larva of the black swallowtail butterfly – but seems otherwise immune to pests and disease. The main problem with parsley is getting the slow-germinating seed to sprout. Although most catalogs say that it takes three weeks, my experience has been that it's closer to four in early spring when soil is cold. I've found two ways to get around this. For spring plantings, I start parsley seed indoors in flats and plant out the young seedlings about the time I plant cabbage. Indoors, in warm soil, the seed usually germinates in two weeks. To speed up outdoor plantings, pouring a fine stream of very hot water over the just-planted seeds seems to knock a week to ten days off the germination time.

Pennyroyal

Mentha pulegium – English

Hedeoma pulegioides – American

The colonists brought pennyroyal with them, but they found it here, too. The English form is a six-inch-high creeping, round-leaved, half-hardy perennial that grows well in moist, semi-shady places. The more erect American form reaches a height of twelve inches, dies out over winter but self-sows freely, and prefers a dry but still partly shaded spot. It is often found in the wild. The main reason for growing pennyroyal both then and now is for its effectiveness in repelling insects, particularly fleas, ants, and mosquitoes. Although the tea is often prescribed in old herbals, it can be toxic in large doses. Pennyroyal was also used as a poultice to treat facial skin lesions and was put into stale (or worse) water carried on shipboard to make the water more acceptable for drinking.

Rocket

Eruca sativa

Even for the ancients, rocket was primarily a salad herb. Its seed was used medicinally, though, and according to Pliny was recommended to help prospective whipping victims to endure the pain.

Reading this, one can't help but think that perhaps we have come a ways after all. Rocket was grown in a bed with other salad herbs, but in general, the planting beds of an eighteenth-century garden were arranged not according to use but by the time of planting. Perennials (flowers, vegetables, and herbs) were grouped together, and all early plantings were made in common beds, again mixing flowers, herbs, and salad plants. (See page 12 for directions for growing rocket.)

Rosemary
Rosmarinus officinalis

If you can find a spot for your rosemary bush near a brick wall, your planting will be both traditional and well protected. The sun's heat, absorbed by the brick, helps to nurture tender rosemary through a mild winter. North of Virginia, bring the pot of rosemary indoors and keep it in a cool sunny place, misting it regularly to provide some humidity. In its native Mediterranean hills, rosemary thrives in rocky, well-drained, rather poor limestone soils. Avoid planting it in over-rich or soggy soil. A tender perennial, rosemary grows into a one- to three-foot-high shrubby form, with thin leaves resembling long hemlock needles. It is usually propagated from cuttings or by layering but may be grown from seed by gardeners well supplied with patience. Sow the very fine seed in flats indoors, pressing them gently into the damp growing medium. When the slow-growing seedlings are one to two inches high they may be transplanted to the herb bed, six inches apart, once the danger of frost is over. A few of the many old uses for rosemary include curing dandruff (as a wash), treating arthritis and heart ailments, and repelling moths. Its subtle flavor in cookery, especially with lamb and pork, is reason enough for giving rosemary a place of honor in the dooryard garden. Once you develop the habit, lamb stew without rosemary is unthinkable!

Sage
Salvia officinalis

Always a much-loved kitchen herb, especially good with pork, poultry, bread stuffings, and cheese dishes, sage was also much relied on for healing. Some of the many troubles it was said to alleviate include sunburn, plague, palsy, cough, childbirth, pain-in-the-side, headache, and overeating. Our amusement over such encyclopedic claims should not obscure the very real virtues of the plant when taken as a tea to relieve headaches and coughs. An elderly patient who was once under my care for a short time would call for a sage leaf fresh-plucked from his marvelous brick-walled garden to slip under his dentures when his gums were irritated. And it seemed to help.

British gardeners plant sage near their carrot rows to discourage the pesky carrot fly.

An easy-to-grow perennial, a mature sage plant is two or three feet tall with gray-green, slighly hairy, one- to three-inch thin, oval leaves. Start with root cuttings or seeds and propagate established plants by layering. They are most at home in a dry, sunny, well-limed spot. Sage is quite hardy, but where winters are severe, set the plants on the warm south side of a building. Don't cut from them after September. Older plants develop large patches of bare woody growth and produce fewer leaves, so you might want to plan on renewing the clump every five years or so.

Savory

Satureia

S. hortensis – summer

S. montana – winter

Savory has a long-standing international reputation for aiding in the digestion of what Gerard called the 'windie pulses' . . . dried peas and beans. In Germany, in fact, it is called *Bohneukraut* – the bean herb. Some gardeners seem to think that the herb also protects bean plants from bean beetles and other pests, but I have not found this to be true in my garden. I'd recommend the annual (summer) savory for your kitchen garden; it is much milder in flavor than the perennial winter savory. The seeds are very tiny but will fare well enough in the open row if you've combed the soil to a fine tilth. Sow them after danger of frost and thin the plants to stand a foot apart. They'll grow about a foot tall, or somewhat less in the really poor soil that probably suits them better. Good drainage, limestone, and full sun will make them feel at home. The first cutting usually has the best flavor.

In addition to tucking a sprig of savory into your next pot of baked beans, you might try the seventeenth-century practice of mixing dried savory with fine bread crumbs when breading veal or other meat. And if you're stung by a bee or other insect, rub a fresh savory leaf on the punctured spot for quick relief.

Tansy
Tanacetum vulgare

Tansy plants, the direct descendants of seed ordered from England by early colonists, grow wild now in many Eastern states. The ferny-leaved perennial plants grow three feet tall, with yellow ray-less button-like flowers arranged in what Gerard called 'clustered tufts' (how could I improve on that?). Tansy was used in five ways: as a medicinal tea, an insect repellent, a liniment (when steeped in alcohol), a vermifuge (just the flowers and seeds for this), and a seasoning (young leaves only) for egg dishes and puddings. Recent studies have shown that tansy has a toxic effect when eaten in large amounts, so I wouldn't recommend making tea or tansy cakes, but that still leaves us with the possibility of scattering tansy leaves in summer garment bags, interplanting the herb in the vegetable garden to scare off insect pests, and using the penetrating aromatic preparation to rub on sprains. Besides, the dried flower heads add color to winter bouquets, and the attractive leaves and bright flowers mix agreeably with other herbs in the bed. Tansy self-sows enthusiastically, but since I could find none in my neighborhood, I started some from seed. Just rake the seeds lightly into the ground in mid spring wherever you want the plants to grow.

Tarragon
Artemisia dracunculus

An elegant, temperamental but especially delicious herb for which — believe it or not — no medicinal claims seem to have been made. It was widely used in salads and is still without peer for seasoning chicken, seafood, lamb, and lettuce, as well as for flavoring vinegar with its subtle anise-like flavor.

Tarragon is supposed to grow eighteen inches high at maturity but I must admit I've never raised any that got that far. Apparently the soil drainage in the spot where I planted them was only fair, and tarragon wants super-sharp drainage. Soil shouldn't be too rich, though, and a little shade is all right. Northern gardeners will need to mulch tarragon and cover it with a box or basket in order to pull it through the winter. In the far north, it should be grown as a pot plant and brought inside for the cold months. Tarragon seldom sets seed, so you will need to buy plants. Root some cuttings of half-hardened branches, not woody but not new and sappy either, to maintain your supply and have some for gifts. The plant is not spectacular in appearance, but once you develop an appreciation for its flavor it seems positively beautiful.

Thyme

Thymus vulgaris; T. serpyllum

The tiny-leaved, branching, mat-like thyme plant is more powerful than it looks. Its use in cough remedies is legendary; in addition, it was administered in the healing of worms, sciatica, hiccups, whooping cough, and (as a poultice) for toothache. Reports of its antibacterial activity, although not backed by any research studies that I can find, seem at least worth listening to. At any rate, the flavor is good. We like pinches of thyme in casseroles, soups, stews, and salads, and I usually pot up a plant or two from the border to provide indoor cuttings during the winter. Thyme is easy to raise from seed. It grows slowly, and stays small, creeping farther than its height. Older plants get woody and produce a scanty supply of leaves, so it's a good idea to start a few new plants from seed once in a while. Seed may be sown directly in the garden, but the plants are so small that I prefer to raise seedlings in flats in the house and then set them out where I want them. If you do have a stony place where foot traffic is not heavy, you might like to try scattering seeds of creeping thyme (*Thymus serpyllum*) between the stones to make an aromatic carpet. All thymes like sun and good drainage, but they're adaptable plants, not hard to please.

Wormwood
Artemisia absinthium

The insect-repellent properties of this woody perennial artemisia seem to be widely recognized. Wormwood tea is recommended as a spray to discourage garden insects and the dried leaves repel moths and fleas. The plant was prescribed as a vermifuge by the early herbalists, and if it didn't help there, it was taken to relieve colic, bruises, and problems with weak stomachs. Since wormwood tea (an intensely bitter brew, by the way) has been known to cause hallucinations, I'd recommend confining your experiments with it to landscaping and insect control. The silvery-gray leaves of wormwood add richness to the textured pattern of the green garden. Start with seeds, cuttings, or root divisions and give the plant the usual sunny, well-drained position that most herbs like. Wormwood tolerates a fairly moist soil, though. In many places in the South it grows wild. If you've grown so much tansy, lavender, and pennyroyal that you don't need any more moth-repellent plants, try wiring dried sprigs of wormwood to a circle of wire to form a charming herb wreath, to which you can then fasten dried pods or little bundles of other dried herbs.

III. Grapes, Nuts, and Snacks

Sweet Grapes

Grapes

Eating dessert in the garden patch is one of our favorite summer traditions. We start with strawberries in June and go on to raspberries in July. In August and September we head for the grape vines. Of all the fruits we munch in the patch, our grapes delight us as much as any. Unsprayed, they need no washing. Neither do they require cooking or peeling. They give up so easily – no stooping or tangling with briars. And they are so beautiful, hanging in clusters of purple, green, bronze, tawny red, the very picture of abundance. All of this – the ease, the color, the gorgeous ripe clusters – would almost be enough. But there's more. There are grapes so delicious that they evoke from all of us an involuntary 'mmm' of appreciation. The superlative flavor in grapes available to today's gardeners is one of the reasons I'm glad to be living here and now.

Grapes have been cultivated for thousands of years, and enjoyed in the wild for countless more thousands before they were tamed. Grapes and man have done well together. Most temperate zones have their native grape varieties.

The standard Eastern grape, the customary dooryard variety, has long been the Concord. Here in Pennsylvania, Concord grapes ripen in early September. Baskets of grapes given away by neighbors are usually Concord. I've never seen anyone give away a basket of Buffalo grapes, though, or Sheridan, or Interlaken. Don't get me wrong; Concord grapes are good – dependable, vigorous, productive. Keep some Concords; they've met the test of time. But don't stop there, for beyond the Concords there is a whole arbor full of scrumptious varieties that aren't any more difficult to grow. Like:

Buffalo, an early purple grape of superlative flavor and aroma, quite vigorous and prolific.

Himrod and Interlaken are fine-flavored green-golden seedless grapes that ripen in August. Both are winter hardy; Interlaken weathers temperatures below zero and Himrod withstands even colder weather.

Concord Seedless, smaller and earlier than the regular Concord, easier for small children to eat and superb in preserves.

Van Buren, an extra hardy purple grape, ripening before Concord and producing fine sweet berries of medium size, vigorous even on poor soil.

Steuben also ripens before Concord and keeps well if you can resist its delicious, aromatic blue clusters.

Catawba bears a late red grape of good quality, also a good keeper.

Alden bears great big juicy, sweet, aromatic grapes on a hardy vine. It is very productive and keeps well.

Delaware, ripening sweet red grapes in mid September.

Niagara, ripening with Delaware, produces a fine, juicy, sweet white grape on a vigorous vine. A good one for covering arbors, as is Concord.

Sheridan ends the season in late September or early October with a most delicious, sweet blue grape that keeps well. The vine is vigorous, hardy, and productive.

If you have a choice of sites for your grapes, a southern slope is ideal for frost protection and the full sun that brings out all the sweetness the fruit can have. Since grapes are wind-pollinated, the vines should be set no more than fifty feet apart, and much closer than that if possible, down to seven or eight feet. (Have you ever smelled a grape blossom? Insignificant in appearance, but very fragrant.)

Since they grow well on a fence and spread in only two dimensions, grape vines fit well into yards that are too small for fruit trees. Several years ago *Country Journal* published a marvelous picture of grape vines growing on a low house roof, an excellent use of space and, not so incidentally, effective natural cooling for the living space beneath.

Our vines are planted by cedar posts spaced eight feet apart. Three strands of heavy wire fastened to the posts support the vines. The posts are set with their heavy ends two feet below ground level. (End posts should be deeper: two and one-half feet at least.)

The vines do not really need permanent support in their first year of growth, but they should have at least a stake for protection and training in the right direction. In the meantime, you can decide on the system you want to use with your grapes and can be preparing and setting the posts accordingly.

At planting time, we pruned the roots lightly to encourage generous development of feeder rootlets and we cut the plant back to three buds. Drastic treatment, but best for the vine's long-term development.

Every year since planting, we have spread manure and wood ashes around the plants, working up to a bushel of manure for the mature three-year-old plants. A well-developed grapevine has roots extending several feet out from the trunk, so all soil enrichment offerings should be extended two to three feet beyond the main stem, more in the case of old vines. The feeder roots are near the soil surface too, so mulching is much to be preferred to mechanical cultivation for weed control.

Grapes thrive in even very dry seasons since their roots penetrate very deeply (as much as eight feet) into the subsoil. If air drainage is poor, mildew may be a problem. For this reason, it is best not to plant rows of grapes closer than nine to ten feet. You want sun and air to reach the plants. Mummified grapes are a sign of black rot. Control this fungus by removing and burning any affected bunches. Japanese beetles show great enthusiasm for grape foliage and in a bad year the vines can look like lace curtains. (See page 210 for hints on controlling this pest.) Damage to the fruit from stinging insects and birds may be prevented by enclosing the grape clusters in paper bags when they begin to ripen.

Pruning of grapes is a contemplative art that is learned as you live your way into it. Some of us suspect that, even as we are guiding the vine, the grape is training us . . . to be observant,

> responsive,
> responsible,
> attentive.

Don't let it worry you; you and the grapevine will grow together.

No matter how natural your garden may be, and we lean to shagginess rather than total control, you won't get far with grapes if you let them ramble on their own. They'll form a wild tangle that produces few and small berries. Pruning is one of the responsibilities man accepts when adopting plants to perfect for his own purposes.

To prune judiciously, you need to know how a grapevine grows. It is the new growth, each season, that produces the fruit. A new cane grows in spring from a bud at each leaf node and bears a bunch of grapes in the fall. By fall, the new cane has hardened and grown a fibrous bark. It will produce fruiting shoots of its own next year. Pruning is a process of selection and of training the best new shoots, always discarding old canes once they have borne fruit. Good pruning develops proper balance between cane growth and fruit yield.

Let's take a vine from planting to maturity and see when and where it should be pruned. At planting time, the vine should be cut back to two or three buds. Let the plant grow over the next season so it can develop good roots. At pruning time (December through March) the first winter after planting, prune off all but the best cane. Reduce that cane to three buds and tie it to a stake or an arbor. During the second spring, new shoots will grow from each bud left on the cane. Retain the strongest one and discard the others. This shoot will develop into the main trunk of the vine.

During the second summer, let the vine flourish tall, nipping out the top of the stem at twelve inches above the top wire support. Tie the vine to its support. Leave the upper shoots to grow out along the wires. Remove those on the lower part of the vine.

At pruning time in the second winter, cut back the side shoots to two-bud spurs. This keeps the growth centralized near the main trunk and prevents unwieldy rambling.

During the third winter pruning, leave two fruiting canes with eight to ten buds and also leave four spurs with two buds each. Other canes should be removed.

During each succeeding winter (and a grape vine can keep going for at least sixty years!) remove all old canes that have borne fruit. Retain the upper shoot of each spur to become the next year's fruiting cane with eight to twelve buds. Cut back the lower shoot of each spur to two buds and keep it as a spur. Choose about five or six spurs and canes each year for retaining on the vine. In other words, you're always thinking two years ahead – developing budded spurs that will bud out the following year into fruit-producing canes. Look for a decent sampling of grapes by the third year and enough to boast about within the following two to three years.

There are other good methods of training grapes. This one works for us.

You may want to try to increase your stock of vines by rooting the clippings you have pruned off. Select good mature canes, about one-quarter inch in diameter. Plant them deeply in a nursery row, with one to two nodes buried and the top one just poking through the soil. Choose cuttings from your most vigorous bushes and be sure to label them, or at least make a garden diagram. Select the best-rooted canes that take and plant them in a permanent place, letting them grow unclipped until they are year-old field-grown plants. Then start the pruning and training process.

Even the grape leaves are useful. We like to add a few to the top layer of sauerkraut in the crock and to any canned dilled pickle. Pickles made with grape leaves are, in fact, noticeably crisper. Don't ask me why, but this old country trick really does work! Rolling chopped meat and rice in a grape leaf gives you a delicious near-Eastern one-dish meal. A grape leaf makes a handy outdoor plate, too, or an attractive base for a fruit salad.

If you like grapes, then, and want the very best . . . grow your own!

Plant a Nut Tree

Black Walnut

We had a head start on nuts here on our farm. Our great hedgerow trees – hickories and black walnuts – had been left to themselves over the years and even enriched by washes of topsoil from the open fields. At the edges of the back pastures, small thickets of hazelnuts bloomed and bore in secret, known only to the squirrels. We even have a mystery – a single butternut we found on a rock along the mountain clearing. We hope the parent tree is on our land; finding it has become a cause, and the object of many pleasant spring and fall hikes over the fields and woods.

You'd think that all this wild goodness would have satisfied us. Actually, it brought home to us the many advantages of nut crops, and we began to see just how much additional nut tree plantings could contribute to our homestead.

Consider what a nut tree could do for *you:* beautify your home grounds, add value to your property, shade your house in summer, and produce a rich harvest of nuts. Most nut trees will bear six to eight years after planting, a somewhat longer waiting period than for fruit trees, which could explain why nut trees have been sadly overlooked by homeowners. Unlike most fruit crops, though, nuts need no processing in order to keep them for winter use; simply store the unshelled nuts in a cool place.

On a small property, nut trees may be planted as shade trees, just as maples and oaks would be used, and as curbside plantings. The smaller almonds and filberts lend themselves to backyard plantings. Because they do take time to mature, I always recommend planting nut trees the very first thing in moving to a new location or starting on a landscaping plan. The trees will grow while you're busy with other things. The first year we moved to our farm, we made time for the planting of young nut trees, even when other annual garden chores were waiting to be done. Now we're glad we did. The young trees are branching out, developing sturdy trunks, and we're plant-ing a second batch of them. We've even picked a few filberts from our three-year-old bushes.

Almond

Amygdalus communis

Although commonly considered tender exotics, almonds may be obtained in a hardy strain, Hall's Hardy Almond, which will grow wherever peaches do well. The tree is, in fact, a cousin of the peach and resembles it closely. The nearly ripe fruit of the almond tree looks like a runt peach. It has a thick skin, a thin layer of pulp, and a large hard-shelled kernel. Trees should be spaced twenty feet apart.

Almond trees are delicate in appearance, seldom topping fifteen feet, and bear masses of pink flowers in early spring. Although the tree itself is hardy, it can get into trouble in far northern climates because of its tendency to bloom early, usually earlier than the peach. Good choices for lawn plantings, almond trees may easily be covered with a sheet if spring frosts do threaten the blossoms. Even if you don't reap a crop every year, you'll get more good food from a hardy almond than you would from a pin oak or maple or many other widely planted lawn trees.

Black Walnut

Juglans nigra

The wild black walnut, in all its variation, is a superior tree, valued for both its nuts and its beautifully grained wood which doesn't warp or shrink. The nuts retain their rich flavor when cooked better than many other nuts. Try black walnut cookies or – our favorite – black walnut waffles. (Just stud your favorite waffle recipe with a fistful of black walnut meats and pass the maple syrup.)

The black walnut is native to every state east of the Rockies. It needs at least 150 frost-free days. Trees in the far South will occasionally bloom too early, before the weather has stabilized enough not to nip the flower buds, but generally the trees are extremely late to leaf out; they are usually the first to lose their leaves in the fall, as well.

Black walnuts like well-drained soil, not too strongly acid. Highly acid soil may be limed (dolomite is good) but don't overdo it, since overliming may block the tree's absorption of zinc. A pH of 6 to 6.5 is good.

Grafted walnuts, available by mail from nurseries, often bear early, at a height of about seven feet. The variety most often found in catalogs, and the one we've planted, is the Thomas. Other grafted varieties include Stambaugh, Ohio, and Sparrow. The Thomas grafted tree commonly bears as early as five or six years, compared to ten years for most seedling trees. Most named grafted trees bear nuts with larger meats and thinner shells than the average wild tree. Some of them even shell out in perfect halves. A fifteen- to twenty-year-old Thomas black walnut will produce about two bushels of nuts, from which you can crack a good twenty pounds of nutmeats . . . worth about sixty dollars at today's supermarket prices.

A fungus disease, walnut anthracnose, causes blackened or shriveled kernels and shows up as round leaf spots on the leaves in early summer, causing early leaf drop. Defend your trees against this fungus by raking and burning any affected leaves and nuts to destroy the spores that would otherwise live over winter.

Blackened or moldy nuts may also be caused by leaving the nuts unhusked for too long, or letting the unhusked nuts remain too long on the damp ground. We've found that the easiest way to husk the nuts is to spread them in the driveway where the car can run over them and split open the husks. If you're in a hurry, you can crack off the green aromatic husks with a well-aimed hammer blow. Wear your best cellar-cleaning outfit to do this job, though, for the brown-staining juice spatters. The dye in the husks will stain your hands, too, unless you wear gloves. Where I live, walnut-stained hands in October are considered the mark of the country person, accepted and understood and often calling forth reminiscences from my elderly friends about the nutting parties of their youth.

Butternut

Juglans cinerea

The butternut, sometimes called the white walnut, is the hardiest northern nut tree. Its range extends well above that of the black walnut. Not a tall tree, except under forest conditions, it is broad with a short thick trunk and many low, heavy branches. Like the black walnut, the butternut grows in a corky husk that has often served to dye fabric brown. Nuts are elongated and roughly ridged, pointed on the end. Their meats, though well hidden, are delicious, milder flavored than the black walnut, although somewhat more prone to rancidity if not kept cool.

Plant butternut trees forty feet from other large trees. While the life expectancy of butternuts is shorter than that of the black walnut or hickory, if the tree lives only forty years it will still bear a good many nuts in that time.

Chinese Chestnut

Castanea mollissima

This imported replacement for the doomed American chestnut bears satin-surfaced, sweet-tasting nuts in husks that bristle with sharp spines. The nuts fall free from the husk when they drop and should be gathered promptly. The young trees are shallow rooted and thus quite vulnerable to drought, but they also need good drainage and should never be planted in a spot where water puddles. Put plenty of humus in the planting hole and mulch the soil surface to retain moisture. Just be sure to keep mulch away from the trunk so mice won't set up housekeeping there and gnaw on the bark.

A single tree will sometimes bear nuts, but not nearly as many as you'll get if you plant two for better pollination. Space them thirty-five feet apart. A mature tree will be fifty to sixty feet tall with a spreading habit. Fully grown trees in warm climates may produce as much as 150 pounds of nuts. Chinese chestnuts usually begin to bear three years after planting and by the sixth year you should have plenty of nuts for chestnut stuffing and several chestnut roasts to boot.

When I was a young visiting nurse working in old South Philadelphia, I would often pass the elderly roast chestnut vendor with his pushcart as I was hurrying home in the early December dark at the end of a busy day climbing tenement stairs. Now when I roast chestnuts in my own country oven, the aroma brings back the city with its worn cobblestones and scurrying crowds, the sharp cold air just before snow, the twinkle in the eye of the old chestnut man, the warmth of the chestnuts juggled in a cold hand. If chestnuts aren't among your memories, they probably will be not too many years after you plant the tree.

I'm indebted to our friends Dick and Betty Parsons for the roasting method that seems to work best. Nick a slit in the shell of each nut. Rinse the nuts in water. Then roast them in a shallow pan in a 350-degree oven for thirty to forty minutes. Perfect! Far superior to my former methods of boiling or steaming them, which tended to make them watery.

Chestnuts, by the way, are 50 percent water, about 42 percent starch, 5 percent oil, and the rest protein. They do not keep as well as other nuts. Plastic-bag storage often encourages mold. Keep them in a paper bag and they'll last several weeks in a cool place.

English Walnut

Juglans regia

The English walnut has been improved tremendously, over the centuries, by simple selection and replanting of superior nuts. If you could compare today's meaty nut with the thick-shelled, poorly flavored nut of the wild tree from which it is descended, you would see how much progress has been made.

Most regular strains of English walnut survive winters as cold as minus 10 degrees F. *Some* winter chilling is necessary in order to promote nut production, but severe chilling will kill the buds. A relatively recent introduction, the Carpathian walnut, is hardy to minus 30 degrees F. Late spring frosts also damage blossoms and affect yield. One year, in fact, a severe late frost made our English walnut tree shed all its leaves suddenly in one day. They grew back, and some late-blooming flowers did form nuts, but the harvest was small that year. Since the English walnut does sometimes bloom rashly early, you might consider planting it on a northern exposure where cool temperatures will foster later blooming. Ours (not a Carpathian) is on a slight southern slope – fine when there is no late freeze, but risky when there is.

A five-year-old walnut tree will begin to bear female blossoms, but the pollen-contributing male blossoms will not show up until the seventh year. This explains the unfruitfulness of young trees with no pollinator tree close by. After the seventh year, the tree may be considered self-pollinating.

English walnuts prosper in rich, well-drained, slightly acid soil. If possible, put a shovelful of compost in the planting hole. You'll never have such a good opportunity again! Plant the trees fifty feet apart.

Filbert

Corylus maxima

The filbert is the cultivated European counterpart of the native American hazelnut. Although slightly less hardy than the hazelnut, it bears larger nuts. This is *the* nut tree to plant for an early crop; most filberts begin to produce nuts three years after planting.

Filberts do well wherever peaches thrive, as long as temperatures do not fall below minus 15 degrees F. The bushes can stand lower temperatures, but dormant buds will be killed.

The filbert's natural form is a shrubby bush. It may be grown as a cluster or a hedge, or pruned to assume tree form. Training and pruning should begin when the tree is very young because the bark is delicate and slow to heal. Smaller twigs will heal over more quickly than large ones. If you want a filbert *tree* rather than a bush, prune off all extra shoots, leaving a single main stem, when planting the young tree.

Space trees twenty-five feet apart, individual bushes ten to twelve feet apart, and filberts for a continuous hedge six feet apart. When planting, dig a deep hole and direct the roots straight down rather than out to the side, to minimize the growth of suckers from the root. The roots will ultimately range to a depth of eleven to twelve feet.

In the fall when loss of leaves bares the bush, you'll notice tassels hanging from the branches. These are the catkins – bearers of next year's flowers. Both male and female flowers appear on a single bush, but you'll need at least two bushes of different varieties because filberts do not accept their own pollen. Royal, DuChilly, and Barcelona are some of the most widely sold filbert strains. If you order three bushes, get two Barcelonas and one DuChilly for pollination.

Our filberts have never been troubled by insects or disease. Their one weakness is the tendency of the catkins to be very responsive to the kind of deceptively mild day that can occur in early March. This early exuberance is sometimes laid low by a hard April frost. Our first planting of filberts, in a sunny sheltered spot, has more than once bloomed early, only to prove unfruitful when a hard frost slid down the mountain and froze out the eager blossoms. The second planting we made, on a western slope that receives some winter shade, has fared much better and started bearing in its second year – only a few nuts, but they were marvelous.

Filberts are easily propagated, either by digging up rooted suckers, or by layering, burying all but the top three inches of a young branch under a three-inch mound of soil. I usually put a rock on the soil mound so the branch won't snap back up. Branches that are layered in spring often form roots by fall. If yours are slow to root, nick the bark with a penknife before covering it with soil.

With their handsome smooth rusty brown shells, filberts are borne in attractive fringed husks which are themselves worth saving for wreaths and dried arrangements. And once you have a crop, no one will have to tell you what to do with it. The nuts are delicious raw. If you must toast them, toast lightly and toss them in a little oil . . . the perfect Continental dessert, with some choice fruit and a wedge of room-temperature cheese.

Hickory

Carya ovata – shagbark

C. laciniosa – shellbark

Both the shellbark and the shagbark form handsome shade trees, achieving an eventual height of 150 feet, although they grow rather slowly. In both trees the bark appears like a loose, shaggy coat of semi-detached strips, most pronounced in the shagbark. Shagbarks are hardy up into Canada, while the range of the slightly more tender shellbark extends as far north as southern New England, south to Texas, and west to Nebraska. The trees are self-fertile, needing no extra pollinating trees, but when one is present, they cross-pollinate freely, resulting in a wide variety of seedling trees. If you're feeling especially adventurous, try growing a few trees from seed by planting the nuts. You can even graft scions from known producing trees to the rootstock of your seedling tree.

Unless you have access to wild seedling trees or nuts, though, you'll most likely begin your hickory growing venture by buying a young seedling tree from a nursery. Be prepared to give it your very best care. The hickory has a strong, deep taproot which must be severed in digging up the tree, making it a somewhat tricky tree to transplant successfully. Dig a generous hole for that unlikely look-ing root and take care not to bend the root when you put the tree in the hole. Fill in the hole with good topsoil and water it weekly when rainfall is scant (less than one inch a week). Once the tree is estab-lished, fertilize it yearly. Trees should be spaced forty to fifty feet apart. Hickories appreciate good fertile soil. They are long-lived trees, and once you've had a taste of the nuts, I'm sure you'll con-sider the effort worthwhile. Hickory flavor is more subtle and ver-satile than that of the black walnut, and at least as good as the pecan, if not better. Just a few hickory nuts added to a bowl of granola make it a very special dish.

Japanese Walnut or Heartnut
Juglans cordiformis ailanthifolia

Relatively new in our country, the heartnut would seem well prepared to thrive in the humid summers of eastern North America. It does well in different climates, from Georgia to Nova Scotia, and in either sandy or heavy soil. Even with its comparatively short thirty-year life expectancy, it is well worth planting as a lawn or specimen tree. Thirty-five feet between trees is ample room for this small member of the walnut family. Heartnuts, similar in flavor to butternuts, are borne in clusters. The shells are smooth and easy to crack. Frost damage is seldom a problem with the heartnut. If peaches grow well in your area, heartnuts should too.

Pecan
Carya illinoensis

One of my husband's colleagues, a native of South Carolina, has the enviable skill of cracking pecans so that the nutmeats come out whole. Apparently he grew up knowing how. Anyone who can do that should have his own pecan tree. When the pecan trees we've planted here begin to bear, we hope to become adept at this art too. Pecans in Pennsylvania? Yes, northern varieties like Major, Indiana, and Colby often ripen nuts by October, given 180 to 200 frost-free days. Southern pecans like Schley, Burkett, and Stuart need 220 to 270 good warm (not just frost-free) days. The hardy northern trees bear smaller nuts with thicker shells than their Southern cousins. Pecan blossoms open fairly late; still, even northern varieties are not always safe from frost. Very sudden, severe freezes may damage not only the blossoms but also the tree. The upper northern range for hardy pecans runs along a line from Pennsylvania through Iowa and Oklahoma.

Although annual crops of pecans are not by any means a sure thing for Midwestern and mid-Atlantic gardeners, the tree is a handsome ornamental and entirely worth its keep as a shade tree. If you're lucky enough to live where pecans thrive without making a Project out of it, feed the trees generously with manure each year, enjoy your good fortune, and practice that arcane cracking art. If you're ever at a loss for gift ideas for your Northern friends, take it from one of them: Make it pecans!

Once you have decided on the particular nut trees you want to plant, here are some hints that will help you get the most from your trees:

Nut Tips

1. Most nut trees have a deep taproot with only a few small feeder roots along the side. Thus they suffer more from transplanting than fruit trees, which usually have an abundance of fine roots. When you plant the tree, clip one-half inch from the bottom of the taproot to encourage growth of feeder roots. Spring is the best time to plant nut trees; fall-planted trees sometimes die when their small, scanty feeder roots die out over winter.
2. If that old saw about the wisdom of putting a one-dollar plant in a five-dollar hole (rather than a five-dollar plant in a one-dollar hole) is so often repeated, that is because it is true. It is especially true in planting nut trees. Dig a generous hole, at least as wide as a bushel basket, and no less than six inches deeper than the depth of the roots. The roots of the tree should fit into the hole easily without crowding or bending.

   Fill in the bottom of the hole with six inches of good topsoil. If you are going to improve the soil by adding several handfuls of bone meal, rock phosphate, greensand, or compost, now is the time to do it. Mix these materials into the loose soil at the bottom of the hole. Now position the tree with its roots spread as much as possible into the loose bottom layer of soil. Next fill in the hole with fine topsoil. Then pour a bucket of water around the tree to settle the soil around the roots. Top off the ground around the tree with another shovelful of soil or two to bring it almost level, but not mounded up. It will sink slightly with the next rain.

   If you are planting a grafted tree, take care to keep the graft union above soil level or the tree may send up suckers from the less desirable variety used for rooting. Set the stake or stakes that you will use to support the tree at the time of planting so that they will not puncture newly formed feeder roots as they might if you added them later.
3. Nut trees are susceptible to sunscald. Protect the trunks by

wrapping them with foil, burlap, or commercial tree-wrapping paper or by whitewashing them.

4. When you can, plant nut trees, particularly the early bloomers, on a north slope to delay blooming and thus lessen the chance of frost damage.

5. Roots of black walnuts and English walnuts exude juglone, a toxic substance which may retard the growth of vegetables, particularly soybeans, beets, and tomatoes. If you have a choice, plant your walnut trees a good sixty feet from your garden. But if you don't have that much space, don't despair. An English walnut tree planted at the corner of my kitchen garden does not seem to have had any ill effect on flowers, peas, lettuce, cauliflower, parsley, and onions I've planted near it, although beets did not do well there.

6. More information about nut trees and access to unusual varieties is available through the Northern Nut Growers Association. (See Appendix A at the end of this book for address.) Some states have nut growers' associations too, which can provide help with local conditions and varieties and often sponsor grafting demonstrations and scion-wood trading events. Your county agricultural agent should know where they are.

7. How can you tell which nuts are empty? Dump them in a pail of water. Those that float are duds.

8. Let the nuts dry for a week or two after husking, before you crack them. Then try a few to see whether they've lost their green' taste.

9. Tough nuts like black walnuts, hickories, and butternuts may be cracked by striking the pointed end with a hammer, crushing in a vise, or using one of the new gear-action nutcrackers – a marvelous invention which cracks the nut without crushing it and releases complete halves in many hickory nuts, and quarters in black walnuts. With a nutcracker like this, a person could even develop a small cottage industry cracking out nutmeats for sale to bakeries, stores, and farmers' markets. We wouldn't be without ours. (See Appendix B at the back of this book.) The man who once owned our farm tells, apropos of the 'good old days,' how his parents would line the children up on winter evenings and they'd all crack nuts, to the point of exhaustion, often far into the night, to sell at the weekly farm market. I can't help thinking how much they would have appreciated our crude but effective nutcracker.

Nutting, both gathering and cracking, can be a delightful social occasion, though, and there is still nothing to compare with the cozy security of gathering around a hot wood stove on a snowbound winter evening with a basket of nuts for cracking. If they are nuts you've grown and gathered yourself, they taste that much better.

If you are already growing all the vegetables you need for your dinner table, why not progress to growing your own snacks, too? These nutritious garden-grown treats are not at all difficult to raise; any one of them would, in fact, be a good project for a child's garden, assuming a bit of adult help is available.

Popcorn
Zea mays everta

If you can grow decent sweet corn, you should be able to raise a fine crop of popcorn. Experience is not necessary for success, though; even if this is your first year of gardening, you may well find that planting popcorn will be one of your more satisfying ventures. Picking time is less critical than for sweet corn, which must be snatched promptly when it reaches its brief moment of perfection. Since popcorn should dry on the stalk anyway, your only picking concern will be to encourage impatient children to leave the ears on the stalk long enough to allow them to cure sufficiently. In order to pop, you see, the kernels must develop a skin hard enough to contain the internal moisture until it builds up enough steam-generated pressure to burst the kernel.

Popcorn has shorter ears and smaller kernels than sweet corn. Some varieties, like White Cloud Hull-less Hybrid, Tom Thumb, and Sno-Puff, have pointed white rice-like kernels which pop to high volume and excellent tenderness. Yellow varieties, some with rounded kernels, are also available. South American Hybrid, for example, produces creamy colored kernels that, when popped, look as though they've already been buttered. Strawberry popcorn is a double-purpose variety grown for both its plump little two-inch ears, which make attractive table and door decorations, and its popable kernels. Almost every seed catalog carries at least one variety of popcorn and since, in our experience at least, there is less flavor difference between varieties of popcorn than sweet corn, you'll find it hard to go wrong on even a random choice. Naturally, varieties grown especially for popping are often more tender and pop to a higher volume than those which are also advertised for their ornamental qualities, but you'd have to be a real popcorn connoisseur to find an objectionable difference.

Plant popcorn about the time of your last frost in spring. Most varieties need ninety to one hundred days to mature. Space seed of dwarf varieties four inches apart, larger kinds eight to ten inches apart. Rows should be two to three feet apart depending on expected stalk height, which usually ranges from three to five feet according to variety.

Like sweet corn, popcorn likes hot weather, well-fertilized and limed soil, and good drainage. It is less particular about moisture and rich soil, though, than sweet corn and, in fact, often produces especially good popping ears in a dry season.

Let the ears remain on the stalk until the kernels are hard and dry. Then pick them, peel back the husk, and hang the ears, bunched together and tied by the husk, in a dry airy place to cure for another week or two. As long as you can protect them from rodents, it is perfectly all right to leave the ears whole until you are ready to use them. Otherwise, flake off the kernels (put an old clean sock over your hand or rub two ears together, to save your fingers). Store the kernels in a covered jar in a cool place. Avoid using artificial heat to dry the ears because the kernels will not pop well if overdried; they won't contain enough moisture to make them burst. If you find that a batch of stored corn doesn't pop well, it is probably too dry. Just shake a few drops of water into the jar and try again in a few days.

Peanuts
Arachis hypogaea

I know no one who's gotten rich planting peanuts north of Virginia, but what's wealth when the aroma of your own homegrown roasted peanuts fills the house? Although peanuts need at least 110 frost-free days, and thrive in really warm weather, they will bear as far north as Michigan, South Dakota, Massachusetts, and central New York state if planted on a southern exposure in sandy soil, which warms up fast. The crops we've grown in the gorgeous deep limestone soil of Lancaster County were, while not outstanding, definitely worth our while. And we know it's possible to do better, because our local feedstore had on display a well-shaped peanut a good two and one-half inches long that had been grown by a nearby farmer, who saves his own seed and selects for size.

Your best bet, though, until you get to be an experienced peanut grower, is to opt for yield rather than size. The small, sweet Spanish peanuts will consistently outproduce the larger Virginia strain when grown in the North.

Sow the seed when your last frost is pretty safely behind you. The maple leaves should be at least the size of squirrel's ears. You can leave the nuts in their shells and poke a shell into soft, deeply worked soil about two inches deep every eight inches. If you prefer to remove the nuts from their casing, take care not to break the skin. Space the shelled nuts three to six inches apart at the same depth, in rows two and one-half feet apart. Thin the plants to stand a foot apart. Some seed will rot and you may have a few gaps in the row. Peanuts do not transplant well.

If it is very important to you to raise peanuts, you might like to try sowing the seed in fiber pots indoors a month or so before planting-out time and setting the plants, pot and all, at one-foot intervals in the row.

When the rather sprawling plants are about a foot high, hill them up by drawing loose soil from either side of the row toward the plant. You'll have more peanuts to pull if you keep the soil around the vines loose and free of crust when flowers form. Peanuts have their own way of doing things, you see. As in other plants, formation of seed (peanuts) follows fertilization of the flowers, but with an extra twist. The yellow flowers, which grow in small groups arising in the leaf axils, actually become buried in the soil as their stalks elongate, after fertilization, to form peduncles which bend them to the ground. The peanuts then grow underground. The nuts form sixty to eighty days after the flower pegs go into the ground.

Although peanuts are often grown on poor soil, they respond to light liming and adequate phosphorus and potassium. What they don't need is nitrogen, which promotes leafy growth and delays seed formation. Since peanuts are legumes, they are capable of utilizing atmospheric nitrogen, thanks to the nitrogen-fixing bacteria that dwell on their roots.

In the South, peanuts are harvested when the vines turn yellow, but northern-grown peanut plants will quite likely still be green when frost hits. Immature peanuts have soft, pale, spongy shells, pale skins, and sometimes a rather bitter flavor. As they mature, shells dry and harden and the skins turn pink and finally red. If the experimental peanut you dig up in September is still immature, wait until frost to harvest the plants so the nuts will have time to mature.

A light frost that just nips the tops won't hurt the underground nuts but they *should* be dug before a heavy, killing frost. When harvested, most peanuts contain about 40 percent moisture. If they are to keep well, they must be dried to a moisture content of around

10 percent. Cure the vines by exposing them to the sun for several days and then hang them in an airy place for several weeks.

Peanuts keep best in paper or cloth bags. Plastic-bag storage encourages dampness and spoilage. The good old southern practice of hanging burlap sacks of peanuts from the rafters can't be beat; it keeps them dry, well-ventilated, and makes the sporting odds higher for marauding mice and squirrels.

Roast and shell the peanuts as you need them. We've found a temperature of 350 degrees F. for twenty to thirty minutes to be just about right. Peanuts are a good source of vitamin E and the B vitamins. Some of those vitamins are inactivated by heat, but the plain raw nuts taste a bit beany. We've discovered, though, that we can have our vitamins and that good nutty taste too. What we do is to roast half the nuts and mix them with an equal amount of raw or lightly roasted nuts. The roasted flavor predominates, and we know the vitamins are there.

Peanuts are especially good candidates for home seed-saving, since the strain will gradually adapt to your particular growing conditions. When saving seed, leave the nuts in the shell until spring, and take care not to split the nut when removing the hull.

Sunflowers

Helianthus anuus

The nutmeat of the sunflower is somewhat less accessible than that of the peanut, but the plant is quite productive and extremely easy to grow. You'll find five or six ornamental types listed in the flower sections of seed catalogs, but for snacking seeds, look in the vegetable section. Mammoth Russian and Peredovik are good varieties, but variety in sunflowers is less important than with many vegetables.

The seeds, often called polly seeds, have a delicious nutlike taste and a good supply of B vitamins and the minerals calcium, iron, and phosphorus. They contain 22 percent protein and 30 percent unsaturated oil. Although it is common practice to roast the bulk-shelled seeds purchased in stores, the kernels are good – and certainly more nutritious – eaten raw.

Sunflowers can be grown in any part of the United States or Canada where corn will grow. Although they require a long growing season – at least 120 days – they withstand light frost in the early seedling stage, and in fact often volunteer in mid spring from crops grown the previous year. We plant our sunflowers around the time of our last frost, dropping a seed every six to eight inches in rows three to four feet apart and thinning the seedlings later to stand two feet apart. If your season is short, you'd be safe in sowing sunflower seed two weeks before your frost-free date, since it may take that long to germinate in cool weather.

A well-nourished sunflower is a spectacular plant – around ten feet tall with large leaves, a two-inch-thick stalk, and a bright yellow flower head. As the seeds develop, the head nods downward with their weight. Heads of the Mammoth Russian generally measure nine to twenty-four inches across. Be sure to cut the heads before birds pick off the seed or shattering scatters it. Then hang the seed-filled disks in a well-ventilated place to cure for several weeks. This drying helps to bring out their nutty flavor. Watch out for mice, though. Their idea of heaven is a barn festooned with easy-to-reach sunflower heads.

After curing, rub the seeds from the head and store them in cans or jars. Save the rough-toothed circular base of the head for use as a disposable scrubber, if you wish.

Now, how do you extract the seed from the shell? The answer, if you grew up in Poland, as my husband did, or in any other Slavic country, is that you don't. You pop the seeds in one side of your mouth, split the shell with your teeth, chew the kernel, and eject the shell, all the while introducing new seeds and relishing them in the same way. This kind of sleight-of-tongue, while obviously culturally acquired, remains completely beyond me and after having admired my husband's performance for more than twenty years, I can only say that I still haven't the slightest idea how to do it. I split the seeds one by one, the slow way, either biting off a thin side or poking it open with my thumbnail. Still, despite our uneven mastery of this Slavic art, we find a pocketful of sunflower seeds a necessary and companionable adjunct to a walk in our woods.

Other gardeners report shelling sunflower seeds by whirling them in the blender or putting them through a coarse food grinder to crack them, then floating off the hulls and straining out and drying the heavier sunken seeds. This is far from the last word in kernel retrieval, though. For a simpler method, try roasting the seeds at 200 degrees F. until they're crisp, which makes them easier to shell manually. What we really need is a neat little gizmo that would do the job mechanically, so that more of us could take advantage of the fifty-bushel-of-seed-per-acre potential of the sunflower plant. It will probably come from some dedicated free-lance inventor, who will promptly become a hero to us sunflower-seed lovers. Meanwhile, we stuff our pockets with seeds and snack away as we hike.

IV. Experiment!

Save Your Own Garden Seed
Try Some Plant Trading
Weeding as an Adventure
Some Perfectly Useless but
   Fun Things to Do in the Garden
An Utterly Random List of
   Little Gardening Experiments
The Transplanted Gardener
What's New in Garden Insect Control

Save Your Own Garden Seed

Eggplant

Saving garden seeds is an adventure that can continue for years, lead to a study of botany, lure you into the side roads of plant breeding and hybridizing, and engender new friendships with other gardeners. There's even the possibility, remote but nonetheless real, of discovering something new or different in the plant world after years of observation and selection of seeds. At the very least, you'll have fresh, free seed for next year's planting.

Many gardeners who begin saving seed solely as a matter of economy soon progress to improving their homegrown strains of vegetables by selection, by saving seeds each year from the most outstanding plants. It is possible, in this way, to develop a strain of vegetable particularly well suited to your climate and soil and at the same time gradually improve the size, flavor, earliness, keeping quality, yield, disease resistance, or insect resistance of the crop by carefully selecting for these qualities or others that may be important to you. Local favorites or heirloom varieties no longer offered by commercial seed houses can *only* be perpetuated by careful saving of seed and periodic replanting to renew the seed stock.

If you intend to collect seeds from your plants, you will probably find it helpful to know something about the seeds and how they came to be. Though they may appear dry and lifeless, seeds are, in fact, alive. Inside each wispy, prickly, smooth, or ridged seedcase there is a living plant embryo. It exists in a state of suspended animation, absorbing oxygen and giving off carbon dioxide at a very low level, measurable only by special laboratory equipment. No matter how tiny the seed, the embryo within it possesses a rudimentary root, stem, and leaves. When the warmth and moisture necessary for germination are present, enzymes and hormones are activated in the seed to direct the unfolding and development of the ready-to-grow root and leaves. When you're storing seeds from one season to another, then, it is important to keep the seeds cool and dry, so that they don't use up any of their limited supply of stored food in a vain attempt at germination before you plant them.

The flowers and fruits that we consider primary crops are, for the plant, a means to an end. Flowers exist to perpetuate the plant. Fruits grow from pollinated flowers to bear seed. In order for a plant to produce seed, the plant's flower must be pollinated. The pollen is released by the anthers, which are the male portion of the flower. Pollen landing on the stigma, the receptive female portion of the flower, travels down the tube-like style to the ovary where it joins with the ovules (eggs) to form the seed or seeds that will produce a new generation of plants. Some flowers will accept their own pollen.

Several of our most dependable garden plants – beans, peas, and to-matoes – have flowers that are self-pollinating. Other kinds of plants must receive 'new blood,' as it were, requiring pollen from a separate plant of the same species in order to form seed. Transfer of pollen from one plant to another is usually accomplished by insects or wind.

Not all vegetable flowers are showy or decorative. The flowers of beets, spinach, and grains, which depend on wind rather than in-sects for fertilization, are small and insignificant. They don't need to attract attention in order to perpetuate the species. In the corn plant the tassel bears the pollen, and each individual thread of silk on the ear, when fertilized by a wind-borne grain of pollen, forms a kernel on the cob.

For your first efforts in seed saving, stick to the annuals (plants that form seed the same season they're planted) or the perennials (plants that bear seed yearly, once they've reached maturity). Save the biennials, which must winter over to bear seed the year after planting, until you've had a year's experience dealing with the easier kinds. (Biennial vegetables includes most of the root crops (except for spring radishes and potatoes): parsnips, turnips, beets, carrots, rutabagas, and the cabbage family: kale, broccoli, cabbage, brussels sprouts, and collards.)

Don't bother to save seed from hybrids unless you're just curious to see what happens. Hybrid plants are highly inbred and their seed, when it is not sterile, produces plants that are almost always infe-rior to the parent plants.

Another factor you'll want to consider is the method of pollina-tion that is characteristic of the plant. Some plants are self-polli-nated, others are pollinated by insects, while still others are polli-nated by the wind. Plants that are self-pollinated will almost always produce seed that will come true – that is, plants grown from this seed will resemble the parents. (I say 'almost always' because there is a very small margin of error – 0.5 percent of plants – in which random crossing by insects may occur.) Self-pollinated plants are your best bet for dependable results in your early seed-saving trials.

1. Self-pollination. The most common self-pollinating garden
   vegetables are:

Beans	Lima beans
Endive	Peas
Escarole	Soybeans
Lettuce	Tomatoes

Peppers are self-pollinating but may also be crossed by insects if different varieties are closer than fifty feet.

2. Insect Pollination. Insects pollinate a large group of plants, including:

Asparagus	Melons
Broccoli	Onions
Brussels sprouts	Parsley
Cabbage	Parsnips
Carrots	Pumpkins
Collards	Radishes
Cucumbers	Rutabagas
Eggplant	Squash
Kale	Turnips

Seed from insect-pollinated plants will come true if no different but closely related flowering plants are planted nearby, but crossing between varieties frequently takes place, especially if the plants are less than 200 feet apart. Cucumbers, for example, cross readily with other cucumbers, melons with melons, and beets with chard, sugar beets, and other garden beets. While neither pumpkins nor squash will cross with cucumbers or melons, they will often cross with each other and with gourds, with interesting, usually edible, often tasty, but hard-to-identify results.

3. Wind Pollination. Wind-pollinated plants like spinach, beets, and Swiss chard can cross over distances of up to one mile. Corn is also wind-pollinated but since the pollen is heavy it doesn't travel as far. For most home garden purposes, 200 feet between different varieties of corn will assure acceptable purity. If you want to avoid even a small percentage of crossing, make that 1,000 feet or plant early and late varieties, which should not shed pollen at the same time.

In order to obtain seed from the very best plants, you will want to observe them, and possibly make a few notes, throughout the season. Consider the plant as a whole, its vigor, yield, disease resistance. Don't make the mistake of saving seed from a single huge tomato growing on an otherwise undistinguished plant. Your seed selection program is more likely to be furthered by the choice of a fruit that is one of many fine ones, even if slightly smaller, on an outstandingly healthy vine. Early bearing, particularly in corn, tomatoes, and peppers, is often a desirable trait to encourage. However, the first fruit to develop must be left on the plant to form ripe seed, so you must forego eating the first fruits of most vegetables and fruits, except those like pumpkins, melons, and winter squash in which the seed is mature when the fruit is ripe. With leafy plants like lettuce, escarole, spinach, and corn salad, you'll want to choose as your parent plants those that are slow to go to seed.

When you've decided which plant or fruit you want to save for your star seed-bearer, tie a tag or strip of colored cloth to it, or drive in a stake, to designate the plant as one that should not be harvested. This is especially important if more than one family member routinely picks vegetables. If you have had problems with raccoons eating your corn, you'd probably be wise to choose a corn plant in the center of the patch, rather than at the edge, to save for seed.

Allow the fruit to remain on the plant until the seed is fully mature. For squash, pumpkins, and cantaloupes, as noted above, seed is fully developed when fruit is ripe. Peppers from which you want to save seed should be red, not green. Tomatoes, cucumbers, and eggplants should be allowed to turn overripe. Pick them when they're just 'over the hill' — too ripe for ideal eating, but not rotten. Zucchini and other summer squash must be left on the plant until they form a hard shell, with coarse tough flesh and well-developed seeds. Seeds of lettuce, carrot, cabbage, onion, and other vegetables in which the seeds fall soon after they are ripe and dry must be gathered promptly before they scatter. Lettuce seed is ready soon after the yellow flower changes to a ball of fluffy down.

Seeds that are dry when you pluck them from the plant should be air-dried on trays or several layers of newspapers for a week or two. Small amounts of bean seed may be removed from the pods by hand; larger harvests may be threshed by beating the beans with a stick or plastic baseball bat and winnowed by pouring them from one container to another in a stiff breeze which will blow away most of the chaff.

Squash, pumpkin, and melon seeds can simply be scooped from the fruit, washed, and air-dried. Pepper seeds seldom need washing. Tomatoes are usually allowed to ferment for a few days to kill the organisms that cause bacterial canker, a seed-borne disease. Just squash the tomato into a glass, add one-quarter cup of water and set the brew where you will see it and remember to check on it. Stir the tomato/water mixture every day for three to four days. It will begin to bubble on the second or third day, depending on the room temperature. On the fourth or fifth day, spoon or pour off the pulp and lifeless floating seeds that have risen to the top, and then strain, rinse, and dry the heavier, viable seeds that have settled to the bottom.

Biennial vegetables like cabbage, beets, and carrots must be stored in sand or sawdust over the winter and replanted in the garden in the spring. When you select roots for storage, avoid the immatu.e half-developed ones and the old, woody specimens. Choose instead the well-developed, table-ready roots that you'd want to serve for dinner. Clip the leafy tops off, leaving a one-inch stub. Keep the roots cool – a temperature of 33 to 40 degrees F. is ideal – and cover them completely with sawdust or sand. Store them in a damp basement or shed. (They may not all make it through the winter.) In early spring, select the roots that are in the best condition and plant them out as soon as the soil can be worked, spacing them at least twice as far apart as they would normally be planted for vegetable production. The seed stalk that will grow as spring advances may need to be staked if it grows tall. Seed of most biennials will be ripe for harvesting in early to midsummer. Parsnips and salsify will winter over in the ground with protective mulch in most areas of the United States and in many gardens where temperatures seldom drop below o degrees F., carrots will also live over.

The various species of plants differ in the longevity of their seed. Parsnip and onion seeds are notoriously short-lived. Pumpkin seed, on the other hand, will often sprout after spending many years in storage. Seed of any variety will be more likely to retain its full genetic viability, and in some cases exceed that expectation, if storage conditions are favorable.

The two enemies of seed viability are moisture and heat. After harvesting, dry the seed in a well-ventilated but not artificially heated spot, and keep the seed dry until you're ready to put it away. Seal the dried saved seed in small bottles, cans, or film containers, or in sealed envelopes kept inside a large can. Label each container as you fill it. Then keep the packaged seed in a cool dry place, ideally between 32 and 41 degrees F.

The following table will give you an idea of the expected life span of some commonly saved garden seeds:

ONE YEAR
Martynia
Onions
Parsnips

TWO YEARS
Corn
Okra

THREE YEARS
Asparagus
Beans
Carrots
Leeks
Peas

FOUR YEARS
Beets
Fennel
Peppers
Pumpkin
Sorrel
Swiss chard
Tomatoes

FIVE YEARS
Broccoli
Brussels sprouts
Cabbage
Cardoon
Cucumbers
Eggplant
Endive
Lettuce
Muskmelon
Radish
Spinach
Squash
Turnips
Watermelon

Try Some Plant Trading

Strawberry

There are plants you can't find in any seed or nursery catalog. Here in my garden, for example, I'm growing an extra-solid, almost-seed-less Italian tomato, a large cantaloupe, German multiplier onions, and dwarf broom corn, none of which I could have purchased through any seed catalog with which I am familiar. Seed for each of these plants came from other gardeners who have kept these strains alive by replanting them and saving seeds.

Seed trading, I've found, is a double adventure, involving the challenge of raising new kinds of crops from seed (and saving that seed again myself to assure another harvest) and the warmth and stimulation of contact with other gardeners in all sections of the country.

I've seen seed trading ads in barter columns in such publications as *Yankee, Troy-Built Owner News and Gardeners Exchange,* and in local newspapers, but my primary source for seeds of heirloom or hard-to-find varieties is the True Seed Exchange. If you've ever wished for seed of an elusive vegetable you remember from child-hood, wanted to enlist the help of other gardeners in maintaining a special heirloom strain of beans or other vegetables that you've been saving and replanting, or if you simply share the concern of some scientists and gardeners for the preservation of locally developed vegetable strains for the sake of saving a great but otherwise unpro-tected wealth of genetic variety, you might be interested in the work of the True Seed Exchange.

A grass-roots organization founded by Kent Whealy of Princeton, Missouri, the exchange currently lists several hundred members and offers home-saved seeds and plants of every description, ranging from hop vines, mung beans, Vietnamese basil, broom corn, sugar cane, and sorghum to high protein corn, special melons and, of course, the standard vegetables that we all depend on: tomatoes, beans, peas, squash, peppers, onions, lettuce.

For a nominal membership fee ($2.00 in 1978) gardeners have the privilege of requesting seed or plants from other members. Usually only a few seeds are given, just enough for a start. Seeds are sent free but those who request plants are expected to reimburse the sender for the postage. With yearly renewal of membership, an annual cat-alog and newsletter is sent to each member.

The spirit and intent of the Exchange is one of sharing and coop-eration in the absorbing venture of preserving old and unusual veg-etable varieties that, for one reason or another, are not propagated commercially and are therefore in danger of dying out. The yearly catalog sent to all members includes listings of flowers and herb plants and seeds as well as vegetables but vegetables are the principal concern of the Exchange and flower listings are accepted only as part of a larger vegetable offering.

On a more local basis, trading of surplus bulbs, plants, seedlings, divisions of perennial flowers, herbs, shrubs, trees, and even garden produce has become a much-awaited feature of many spring and fall fairs. A woman's club in a town not far from us sponsors an annual plant-trading day. Town residents as well as club members arrive with boxes of iris rhizomes, peony clumps, rhubarb roots, tree seedlings, houseplants, and other garden treasures, and leave with the same cartons jammed with lilac bushes, seedling mulberry trees, wildflowers, ferns, and pots of chives. Everyone is happy. Sometimes an entry fee is charged to defray club expenses or even to add to the group's treasury. There's an old saying among gardeners that the plant for which you thank the giver will not prosper. Perhaps the plant exchange has the answer for that old taboo. Certainly the mutual satisfaction that fills the air at a good plant-trading event makes formal thank-yous irrelevant.

A whimsical, warm-hearted gardener's gesture that I've occasionally encountered is the giveaway. You know how we gardeners hate to toss out perfectly good plants, even when it is evident that ruthless thinning is needed in the perennial bed. Some of us, in fact, develop a reputation for pressing extra plants on everyone who opens the front gate. The solution to this dilemma, pioneered by several imaginative suburban gardeners, is to put out a carton of your extra plants with a large sign on it: FREE PLANTS, HELP YOURSELF. Kind of like a large-scale, free-for-all May basket.

Certain seed companies offer free seed in exchange for seed you've gathered either in the wild or from your garden. The specialized companies that offer this option generally do so in the hope of increasing their stock of hard-to-obtain wildflower seeds or good localized strains of popular vegetables. In most cases, you'd be wise to send for the special printed instructions that are usually provided by these companies, either in their catalog or on separate papers especially printed for would-be seed gatherers. Names of companies following this policy are included, with an appropriate notation, on the list of seed suppliers in the Sources section at the back of this book.

There's another, even simpler, way to obtain plants for which you may be searching. Post signs on food market bulletin boards offering to trade your surplus plants for varieties you need. I've had good luck in locating strawberry, rhubarb, and Jerusalem artichoke plants, as well as trees and shrubs, by tacking up these informal offers on community bulletin boards. An extra dividend has been the delightful opportunity to meet other gardeners and admire their plantings. Instead of waiting for a special catalog or event to bring you what you want or need, see what will turn up when you take matters into your own hands.

Weeding as an Adventure

Dandelion

Weeding is surely regarded as one of the more humdrum aspects of gardening. Most people I know would rank this necessary chore well below seed catalog study or planting or picking, on a scale of delight.

Weeding *can* be an adventure, though. When you kneel in the row and focus your attention on one small space of ground at a time, you find yourself viewing your cultivated patch in a more intimate manner. You notice the first delicate shiny green pea pods, still bearing a dried flower at the pointed end. You see the tomatoes coloring up, the dill feathering out. You get to know how the plants grow, the turn of the stem, angle of leaf, attachment of fruit. You hear the bees in the squash blossoms, smell the sun-warmed herbs, feel the quality of the soil from which you're pulling weeds. And you discover other things you might otherwise have missed.

Volunteer Plants: Self-Sown Seedlings

One of the great pleasures of gardening, for me, at least, is that of finding useful volunteer plants among my carefully arranged rows. Some of these seedlings can be traced to lettuce or tomato plants that went to seed last year. Others, like the pumpkins, squash, or fruit trees, probably reached the garden by way of the hen house; the fruit and vegetable scraps we feed our hens in winter enrich the straw bedding in their pen. We spread the straw on the garden in the early spring. The most puzzling of all, and those that are the most fun to try to trace, are the mystery plants that appear from nowhere — the grapevine, asparagus, barberry hedge, yew bush, walnut and linden tree seedlings that have blown in or have been dropped by birds or buried by squirrels.

What do you do with these volunteers? I consider them an extra dividend, and can usually find a use for them. Often I transplant grape or tree seedlings directly to a protected hedgerow where I can keep an eye on them while they grow bigger. A special nursery row right at the edge of the garden is another good way to nurture young seedling trees and bushes that have found you. You might even discover, as one enterprising gardener did, that these free plants will provide the nucleus of a small ornamental nursery from which started plants can be sold on a casual basis.

Since many fruit trees are cross-pollinated, seedling fruit trees will seldom resemble their parents. They may still be very good, though. Two friends to whom we've given peach tree seedlings insist that the trees bear the best fruit they've ever had. Seedling fruit trees are also well worth keeping as grafting stock, to which you can graft scion wood of known varieties.

Volunteer vegetable seedlings offer a short-term bonus. Although a few kinds are of doubtful value, most are useful if they're not in the way, and some may even be transplanted to grow where you want them. The following are the vegetables most likely to volunteer in the average garden. Watch for them!

ASPARAGUS

Here's a case where the volunteer seedling, even one flown in by birds from a wild plant, is every bit as good as the cultivated crop. Add asparagus seedlings to your perennial patch or use them to start a new bed. Look under trees where mockingbirds roost. I've found enough seedlings in one season to start a whole new bed from volunteers clustered under several favorite bird perches.

CORN

The corn volunteers you find are usually from an ear of sweet corn you overlooked last August, although they can also come from popcorn or field corn that found its way to your garden. Corn cross-pollinates so the seedling will likely be a maverick. And, unless there is other nearby corn in tassel at the proper time, the seedling won't have a chance to be pollinated. It may never bear an ear. Hoe it out and let something else grow there. Corn can't be transplanted.

DILL

Once you plant dill, you'll always have it. Since I depend on the feathery-leaved plant to produce both early green snippings and later flower and seed heads for pickling, I always plant some, even though I know that one of the delights of working the garden in May is the discovery of seedlings from last year's dill. Early planted spring dill will, in fact, set seed which produces volunteer plants in late summer of the same year. Dill forms a taproot and resents transplanting unless done very early and with considerable care.

LETTUCE

Every year at least one leaf lettuce plant gets away from me and sends up a seedstalk. I usually let it go, for the randomly scattered little early lettuce rosettes often appear between the sowings I've made and since they may be plucked early, they will not interfere with main-season plantings. They may also be transplanted. Lettuce is self-pollinated and the seedlings will be like the parent.

PEA

Pea volunteers look big and strong and hopeful but they seldom get the support they need and usually amount to nothing. When they do produce peas, I usually find them too late. They don't transplant well, either. My advice is to turn under young chance pea seedlings as a green manure crop.

POTATO

There's something almost too good to be true about knobby little new potatoes that have sprung from nothing more than a handful of vegetable peelings. While potatoes grown from peelings will never win any size prizes, they are very good indeed. Plants that spring from buried whole green or partly spoiled potatoes are often as good as any in the potato patch proper. They don't transplant well. I usually keep potato volunteers to see what they'll do. The extra helpings of little new potatoes they produce are a pure bonus.

RADISH

Beware. Radishes can cross with wild members of their family (*Crucifers*) to produce worthless weeds that look like radishes when they first sprout. These radish imposters can be host to annoying infestations of destructive flea beetles, tiny round black pinhead-sized beetles.

NEW ZEALAND SPINACH

This thick-leafed hot-weather spinach repeats readily from self-sown seed. Since just the leaves are plucked in midsummer, plenty of flowers remain in the leaf axils and those go on to produce seed, which germinates best at cool temperatures. Although the plant doesn't really get off the ground until warm weather, the seedlings often appear as early as April. Transplant the seedlings only when very young, if at all.

SQUASH AND PUMPKIN

Cross-pollination between pumpkin, gourds, and summer and winter squashes accounts for some of the funny impossible-to-classify freaks you may find in a volunteer pumpkin patch. Such vegetables are edible, though not always as tender and good as their parents. Experiment and see what you think. Volunteers also come true-to-type sometimes. You just never know. If you have plenty of space, let them ramble and see what they produce. Otherwise, grub them out. They don't transplant well.

SUNFLOWER

Volunteer sunflowers, as a whole, often outperform our intentional plantings. Perhaps only the most vigorous seeds survive the winter. The seedling plants do not transplant well, so your best bet is to simply weed out those that come up in inconvenient places. Some of the choice seedlings, on the other hand, may prove to be appropriate in the random locations they've chosen, by the back fence, the bird feeder, or the mailbox, for example.

SWISS CHARD

While this plant doesn't actually volunteer as a self-sown seedling, it does often reappear in the garden the year after planting, much to the surprise of gardeners who have not yet had occasion to be in awe of the staying power of its deep, strong root. Later in the season it will go to seed, but not before you've had a chance for some good early spring pickings of its tender fresh greens.

TOMATO

Despite the frost-tenderness of the seedling, the seeds can and do survive severe winter cold and germinate in late spring when the time is right. Tomato volunteers from seed of regular open-pollinated varieties like Rutgers, Sunray, Marglobe, and others will grow true to type. Those from hybrid plants, however, will be different from the parent, and most likely inferior. The seedlings transplant well and may be used either to fill a gap in the row or to stretch the fruiting season since they come into bearing a bit later than pre-started transplants.

Edible Weeds

Weeding serendipity can yield yet another dividend: edible weeds! With all that has been written in recent years about foraging for wild foods, it is surprising how few gardeners have ever really sampled the wild greens that grow unbidden in their garden rows. Some of these plants, according to studies made by Penn State University food scientists at the urging of wild foods expert Euell Gibbons, and reported in his book *Stalking the Healthful Herbs*, contain more vitamins A and C than many comparable garden crops. If you've ever thought that you'd like to try a bit of foraging, why not begin in your own backyard, with several easily identified garden weeds?

The following weeds are common enough to be found in most parts of the United States, and sufficiently fine flavored to make them worth recommending as potherbs. For help with identification and more information about additional edible garden weeds, consult one of the sources listed in the bibliography at the back of this book.

CHICKWEED *Stellaria media*

The lowly chickweed is loaded with vitality. It is one of the few green plants that contains a significant amount of copper. The crawling, weak-stemmed mat of one-fourth to one-half-inch leaves, with its tiny white star-like flowers, makes a worthwhile addition to the salad bowl or soup pot. The bland-flavored leaves will, in fact, help to tame the strong flavor of other wild or cultivated pungent greens.

DANDELION *Taraxacum officinale*

Bane of the careful lawnkeeper, the dandelion has long been a valued food in many lands. Every part of the plant is edible – root, leaf, bud, flower. Some unsung improviser has probably even found a use for the fluffy seedball. The leaves are the most consistently useful part; they have an agreeable flavor that often prompts an annual spring craving in those who have endured a winter without them. I start picking the leafy rosettes as soon as they're large enough to slide a knife under and continue to pick them until the plant is in bloom, when the leaves turn somewhat bitter. Dandelions grown in good garden soil are often more luxuriant than those in lawns or on road-sides. The roasted root makes an acceptable coffee substitute and the flower buds are delicious briefly steamed and buttered. You can even use the blossoms to make a classic old-time wine to go with the traditional Grandmother's vegetables you may be growing.

DOCK *Rumex crispus; R. obtusifolius*

This perennial relative of buckwheat and rhubarb has a deep, strong taproot that supports it through the winter. Narrow-leaved dock has long, lance-shaped leaves with wavy curled edges springing directly from the ground-hugging crown. Broad-leaved dock has shorter, three- to five-inch-wide leaves that often have reddish veins. Both are on the leathery side but quite tender and good when cooked. Once the seed stalk appears, though, leaf bitterness increases.

LAMB'S-QUARTERS *Chenopodium album*

The one- to two-inch-long leaves of this 'wild spinach' are shaped like a goosefoot and the leaf surface has an unmistakable whitish sheen, especially on the underside. In late summer, some plants have reddish or purple-freckled leaves. When four to twelve inches tall, the whole plant may be picked for salad, soup, or steamed greens. Later, as the weed grows toward its full four- to five-foot height, I like to pluck individual leaves to add to the soup pot. This tender, mild-flavored wild delicacy actually contains almost half again as much vitamins C and A as its tame relative, spinach. I am never sorry to see lamb's-quarters in my garden; in fact, I've come to depend on it for an early spring vegetable.

PIGWEED *Amaranthus retroflexus*

Seedlings of this robust, three- to six-foot-tall plant appear in the garden all season long. The oval, two-inch-long leaves are slightly hairy, best served as a steamed vegetable or in soup rather than salad. The flavor is mild and quite generally acceptable. Pluck seedlings up to one foot tall. Even when young, they have the characteristic red-tipped root of the pigweeds. The root is not edible, but the leaves and the seeds that follow the woolly green flowers are good.

PURSLANE *Portulaca oleracea*

Cousin to the ornamental garden flower portulaca, purslane is a sprawling plant with fleshy stems and thick rounded leaves. It has been cultivated in Middle-Eastern gardens for centuries. The flavor of purslane is mild and agreeable. Try serving the leaves in a tossed salad, steaming the whole plant, or pickling the stems. Be sure to rinse the plant well before cooking, though, for it harbors plenty of gritty soil-surface particles because of its low-slung growing habit.

WINTER CRESS *Barbarea vulgaris*

Gardeners who have tried these 'wild mustard' greens that appear in fields and cultivated ground in early March usually look for them the following year. Picked while nights are still cold, the six- to eight-inch-long lobed leaves are crisp and tasty, with just enough of an authoritative flavor to make them interesting. Later, when weather moderates and blossoms appear, the leaves will taste strong. But the blossom buds, steamed for five minutes and served with butter and a pinch of thyme and marjoram, are one of our favorite early spring dishes, one that we can usually enjoy before most of our garden seeds have germinated.

A neighbor of ours was fond of quoting the maxim Pull ten weeds a day.' Together we would smile at the subtlety of this old saying. Who could stop at ten weeds? Setting this goal for ourselves, though, meant that we got out there in the row and heard and saw and smelled what was going on in the garden. We were only going to pull ten weeds, so we were less likely to procrastinate. We did pull ten weeds, of course, and often went on to yank one hundred more.

And when some of those weeds were good edible fare as nutritious as any of the conventional vegetables we'd planted, why, then we smiled again as we realized we'd reaped a double dividend from a single piece of ground.

Other things have turned up in my garden rows, too, found objects like old coins, bottles, forks, shards of old china plates I ached to have whole, arrowheads, animal jawbones, and the paring knife I had throught was gone forever. You never know what you'll find next. Still, on reflection, it seems to me that the heightened sense of depth and detail that comes from looking close and making small-scale perceptions while weeding is as valuable as any find you can tuck in your pocket or picking basket.

Some Perfectly Useless but
Fun Things to Do in the Garden

Harvest Figure

Gardening is pleasurable work that is, at the same time, recreation. If it yields useful or edible or ornamental dividends, that is, for the true gardener, pure bonus. It is the *process* of working with plants that is rewarding. And so the spirit of playfulness has its place in the garden. I'd like to tell you about a few perfectly useless pranks that are fun to do. If you have a child or a young neighbor or relative for whom you can do some of these things, you'll have a ready-made alibi. If you don't, get in touch with the child in yourself and enjoy the luxury of doing something just for fun, with no serious or profitable purpose in mind.

Cuke in a Bottle

The first trick is the easiest. Anyone can do it, even a child. Simply select a young, straight cucumber growing on a healthy vine. Leaving the cucumber attached to the vine, carefully insert it into a narrow-necked bottle or canning jar. Tuck the bottled cucumber back under the leaves so that it doesn't cook in the sun. Leave the trapped fruit undisturbed for several days, and then check it daily or every other day. You will, of course, have a mystifying exhibit of a large cucumber filling the seemingly impossible confines of a narrow-necked container. If you've used a standard neck quart canning jar, you can pour in your favorite vinegar/spice solution and pickle the cucumber right in the jar. To get it out for eating, you'd have to commit mayhem, of course, but meanwhile you would have had a lot of fun amazing your young visitors and non-gardening friends.

Personal Pumpkin

Children think it's fun to personalize a pumpkin. When the fruit is about half-grown, you see, you can carve your name (or someone else's name, or a message or design) in the still-tender skin of the pumpkin. Use a sharp knife and make a V-shaped cut about one-fourth inch deep and one-eighth to one-fourth inch wide. The growing pumpkin will heal over the cut, making a scar-tissue outline of your name. The cut must be more than a mere scratch, but not so deep or wide that rot sets in.

Butterbean Tent

Then there's the butterbean tent. Lucky the child who can remember hiding out in the tent formed by the bean vines and their poles! The buzzing warmth of a summer day, the small secret hideout, the knowing green of the sheltering vines, all blend in memories of that dreamlike world where days were long and summers endless.

The simplest, one-person tent is formed on the base of a three-pole tepee. Ram the thick end of each bean pole about a foot into the ground and tie or wire the top ends together. The poles should be spaced three to four feet apart if you're using three. You might also try constructing a tepee of six or eight poles spaced eighteen to twenty-four inches apart. Plant five pole bean seeds at the foot of each pole. The vines will climb the poles and form a leafy canopy by midsummer. To create a doorway space, tie a one-inch-diameter stick in a horizontal position between two of the poles, about halfway up the poles, and plant no seeds in the doorway space. (When using closely spaced poles, of course, you'll need to leave a gap of at least two, and preferably three feet between two of the poles to leave room for entering the structure.)

Pole beans are traditional with this kind of summerhouse, but you might prefer to plant seeds of morning glories, climbing nasturtiums, moon vine, gourds, scarlet runner beans, or perhaps a mixture of these.

To make a somewhat roomier hideout, yet one that costs much less than a wooden playhouse and is easier to construct than a tree house, proceed as follows: Set poles in the ground in either circular or rectangular shape, placing two of them a bit closer together than the others, to form a space which will be the doorway. Wire or staple wide mesh wire poultry netting to the poles to form the base of the structure. If you want a roof, tie strings across the top opening. Then plant seeds of any quick-growing vine at the base of each pole. The vines will transform the bare wire and string into a lovely leafy teahouse – ephemeral, but perfect of its kind and for its purpose while it lives.

Squash Trumpet

For the housewarming, you might want some improvised horns. You can gather them in the garden if you're growing squash. As you've probably noticed, the stem of a squash leaf is hollow. To make a trumpet of it, just cut the stem off the vine and make another cut across the solid end of the stem where it joins the leaf. Then cut a slit in the stalk about one-half inch from the solid end. Put this end of the stalk in your mouth and blow on it. Experiment with slit size and stalk length and keep trying if you can't produce a sound on the first try.

Harvest Figures

Those lolling pumpkin-headed leaf-stuffed homey people-forms called harvest figures you see on porches in the fall are fun for everyone – children, gardeners, neighbors, and passersby. Many of us adults, I know, take a not-so-secret delight in putting together these vegetable creations, ostensibly for the kids, but really just as much for ourselves.

No rules govern the construction of harvest figures, unless you count the unwritten but widely accepted dogma that they should be made entirely of found objects – some would insist solely out of garden produce and woods and fields findings. One would not, say, go to the store to buy a mask or hat for one's harvest figure. Never. The pleasure of the art lies, rather, in seeing the grotesque or scary or amusing or clever or even pathetic possibilities in what you do have, at season's end, in surplus from garden and fields. Pumpkins are basic. They usually form the heads. Paper bags, pillow cases, discarded plastic jugs, and even wooden shingles make good heads, too. Bodies are often leaf-stuffed bags clothed in cast-off coats or shirts. Legs may be sticks, iron pipes, long-necked pumpkins, leaf-stuffed stockings or straw-wadded trousers, or perhaps cornstalks or brooms.

You can hang your harvest figure from a tree, lean it against the porch wall, prop it by a lamppost, or construct a group of figures in the front yard. Clothespin fingers, carrot noses, pepper ears, mop or corn-silk hair, are all details that others have used. I maintain, though, that as a true folk art this one should evolve from what occurs spontaneously to you, rather than from what others have done, so I'll not give any more hints. The rest is up to you. Make some silly people and have fun doing it.

An Utterly Random List of
Little Gardening Experiments

Scarecrow

I have a friend who makes a ritual of asking, each spring, 'What's new in your garden this year?' She knows that I can't resist trying unfamiliar patterns, old forgotten techniques, new varieties and combinations in my garden. Every year is different in a garden anyway, of course. Vagaries of weather, even without slight alterations in care from year to year, ensure that no two years will be alike. But I like to shake things up even more. Besides trying new kinds of vegetables, some of which have become family favorites, I like to carry on little experiments in row arranging, studied rule-breaking and just-for-fun plantings.

Perhaps you'd like to try some of these little experiments. If you habitually plant lettuce in straight single rows, assume that no root vegetables can be transplanted, grow flowers mainly for their colors, or order from a single seed catalog, try dipping into the following list of suggested projects. You will find that there is more than one way to accomplish many gardening tasks; that you will gain in authority, confidence, and daring when you discover that a hunch you followed really does work; that you can structure your garden to suit yourself, rather than some arbitrary conventional pattern; that all things – rocks, trees, weeds, and soil, moon and seedlings, sun, vegetables, flowers, insects, birds, and you – are related parts of a great whole that we glimpse from limited but varying angles as we dig, pick, eat, weed, study, and just be in our gardens.

What will you try first?

1. Plant a fragrance garden, including, perhaps, some of the following fragrant flowers:

> Dianthus
> Freesia
> Hyacinth
> Lily of the valley
> Mignonette
> Nicotiana (fragrant at night)
> Old-fashioned roses
> Petunia (fragrant at night)
> Phlox
> Stock
> Sweet peas

And foliage plants:

> Bee balm (bergamot)
> Lavender

> Mints
> Rose geranium

And shrubs:

> Daphne (not hardy north of Washington, D.C.)
> Lilac
> Mock orange
> Oleander (*Nerium odorum* – not hardy)

2. Try talking to your plants, or singing to them. (Quite apart from the 'good vibrations' singing sets in motion, the carbon dioxide you breathe out will do the plants good.)

3. Plant several different kinds of early leaf lettuce in a small three- by three-foot bed, patchwork fashion, with squares of Black-Seeded Simpson, Oak Leaf, Salad Bowl, and other kinds contrasting in color and texture.

4. Transplant some beet and turnip seedlings. You'll get away with it more often if you clip off the large top leaves, nip off the end of the long trailing root, replant promptly, water thoroughly, and shade well for several days.

5. You already keep a compost pile? Good! Why not start a second or a third one to assure a continuous supply. If you have no compost, then start some.

6. Pick vegetables at the end of the day when their above-ground parts have the highest vitamin content and freeze or can them in the cool of the evening.

7. Turn the herb chart to the wall and conduct your *own* trials, relying on taste to determine which foods go well with basil, rosemary, thyme, marjoram, chervil, and other herbal favorites.

8. Order at least one new seed catalog, and try a flower and vegetable you've never grown before.

9. Keep your old favorite varieties of bean, carrot, beet, and other garden staples, but try a different strain, side-by-side, to see how they compare.

10. Make a small raised bed by digging up a three- by four-foot plot thoroughly, adding two bushels of compost and your favorite fertilizer, and shaping edges firmly at an angle (or enclose the bed with boards). Plant vegetables in a solid block; you can weed and pick from all sides.

11. Plant a vegetable or two in the front yard. Some good candidates would be: eggplant, pepper, Chinese cabbage, cherry tomato.

12. Grow a vegetable to please a special friend – burpless cucumbers, perhaps, or super hot peppers or fat little Halloween pumpkins to make some of your young friends happy.

13. When you harvest a head of cabbage, leave the stump in the garden row. Rudimentary buds, usually visible on the stalk when you've picked the solid head, will develop into three or four small, often (but not always) solid heads which will keep you in soups and salads without the trouble of replanting.

14. Start an herb garden, as you promised yourself you would!

15. Put in a cover crop of annual rye grass in a section of the garden where vegetables have finished bearing and plow or dig in the grass early the following spring to improve the soil.

16. Still an armchair gardener? Find a corner of your yard that you can make productive, try container and windowbox gardening, or hunt up a community garden where you can rent a plot. Make it happen!

17. Use a saltshaker to sow small seeds.

18. Try wide-row planting. Many vegetables do well planted in bands four to twelve inches wide, rather than in single-file rows. Try lettuce, carrots, beets, beans. For peas you can make the row as wide as three feet. Weed carefully in the beginning. When vegetables develop, their leaves will help to shade moisture in and weeds out.

19. If you've always staked tomatoes, or always let them sprawl, try using the opposite technique. Or treat yourself to several three-foot-high cylinders of sturdy wire to cage in and support your tomato plants.

20. Make a scarecrow.

21. Enter some of your best garden vegetables in your regional farm and garden fair.

22. For large, clean, easy-to-harvest potatoes, try growing them in mulch. Place seed potatoes on a four-inch bed of straw, leaves, or rotted hay, and cover with another ten inches of mulch, adding more as plants grow and initial layers pack down.

23. Make a cold frame by hinging a discarded window sash section to a south-slanting three- by six-foot wood frame (or whatever dimensions fit your window).

24. Try planting by the moon, just for fun! How does it work? Very briefly, sow seed of root crops when the moon is waning, preferably in the third quarter. Above-ground crops, including leafy plants and those that bear fruit and seeds, are said to

prosper when planted or transplanted while the moon is waxing. The fourth quarter is generally considered, by serious moon-sign planters, to be a barren time, but ideal for weeding, mending, and putting things in order. Moon planting, as I see it, is solid folklore that is difficult to refute, even though some aspects of the practice seem contradictory or superstitious. If you're looking for a gardening experiment that couldn't hurt and costs nothing, here's a place to start. If you become interested, you'll want to read more about the nuances and some of the exceptions to this age-old planting system. (See bibliography for books on this subject.)

25. Make 'manure tea' for summer feeding of leafy plants. How? Either suspend a burlap bag half full of manure in a barrel or can of water or simply stir a shovelful of manure into a pail of water and let the mixture steep for several days. Dip off several quarts into a bucket and dilute with water until the liquid is the color of tea. Refill the main brew with water as the liquid level goes down; it should be good for at least a month.

26. If your soil is heavy clay, adding lime to it will loosen its structure by coagulating the extra-fine particles into larger clumps. Lime is, in fact, more effective than sand, which will often simply bind the clay into a cement-like mass.

27. Tired of chasing errant seed packets all over the lawn? Staple them to the stakes you use for row markers.

28. Some vegetables that are customarily cooked are also good eaten raw. Eat some raw peas right in the garden row – one of the lucky gardener's spring perquisites. Sample some raw asparagus and snap beans right in the patch. Slice young turnips and broccoli and cauliflower florets into the salad. Zucchini, too.

The Transplanted Gardener

Iris

Every year thousands of gardens change hands, for many reasons. People transfer to new jobs, their housing needs change, they seek a variation in climate, or perhaps they finally find the country place of their dreams.

There's no denying that moving is often a wrenching experience. Apart from the regret at leaving friends and familiar haunts, there is the poignant question of the garden in which you have invested so much care and time. Your first impulse is, perhaps, to cart it all – perennials, topsoil, and trees – off to your new home. You wonder and worry whether the new owner will remember to thin the iris, prune the grapes, mulch the orchard trees. You mentally recount the bushels of leaf mold and manure that you have dug into your soil. You compare the bare yard in your new place to the luxuriant landscaping you've achieved at your old home.

But then you remember that moving is an adventure, too, and that starting a new garden will be a satisfying part of that adventure. The long-term plantings you've put in were made for the future, with an acceptance of all its possibilities. Now the fruit trees you've started will feed another family, and you'll soon plant more in a new place.

This, at least, has been our pattern of thought, in the five household moves we've made, each time leaving behind a lovingly tended garden (from which we've often been able to take started plants for our new yard) and planting a new one at our new address.

We have, in fact, gone to what some would consider rather ridiculous lengths to transfer the best of the old garden to our new residence. On our first move, for example, from the little old Philadelphia house we had bought the year after our marriage, to another old house on a tree-lined street in a small Indiana town, we loaded the back seat of our car with cans and cartons of perennial transplants – rhubarb, coral bells, columbine, lily of the valley, chrysanthemums, and more. Our first journey to our new town was a house-hunting trip, during which we kept our precious plants in the motel bathroom with the lights left on. Then, when we'd decided on a house, we asked the owner's permission to plant our flowers and vegetables in an out-of-the-way corner in the yard, so they'd be there waiting for us when we returned with children and household goods.

One of our other moves was more complicated because we sold our old residence and moved to our new town in June, then spent the following four weeks camping while searching for a country place to buy. When we couldn't seem to find a property that was right for us, we decided to rent a house for a year to leave us free to buy our dream homestead when we found it. So that time, the only treasures we could bring from our former home were the few flower seeds that had ripened early, and other seeds saved from former years.

During the month we spent between homes, I missed working with the soil. But I was surprised to find that my appreciation of others' gardens was keener when I had none of my own; their Shasta daisies seemed larger, their columbines more rainbow-colored, when I was not half-consciously comparing them to my own, or smugly thinking 'My peas are ahead of those!' Perhaps I needed this chance to appreciate beauty beyond my own yard, beauty not of my 'making' or owning; to admit the wonder of all growth, even when I hadn't done the planting.

The spades and forks weren't off the moving van long, though, before we had them in the ground. In fact, we had our garden planted before most of the cartons were unpacked. Six weeks after moving into our rented home on July 3, we were eating our own zucchini, cherry tomatoes, lettuce, chard, beet tops, dill greens, and radishes. Soon after that, beans were on our table, followed by full-sized tomatoes, beets, carrots, cabbage, and brussels sprouts.

Planting as we did, late in the season, called for a slight modification of usual practices. We planted seed in shallow furrows, watered well, and then pulled dry soil over the seeds. This helped to prevent crust formation.

When planting the vegetables, I reserved a row for some perennial seeds: gaillardia, Shasta daisy, and Platycodon. The thrifty little plants made a good start for the flower border I developed the following spring.

At the greenhouse where we bought the tomato plants, we also chose an appealing array of geranium, petunia, and ivy plants, and arranged them in a great big clay pot on the front step. This instant welcome garden was worth its weight in gold for the sense of home that it gave us. Visitors and neighbors seemed to appreciate it, too.

Those who are moving directly to their new home would probably be wise to concentrate on soil improvement and tree planting the first year. Cover cropping, manuring, and planting of deeply rooted plants will pay off the following year in better produce and brighter flowers. When planting trees, berries, and grapes, we would discard all poor soil dug from the hole and fill in around the roots with the best soil on the place.

As we plant anew and put down new roots, we begin to see that transplanting can be stimulating to gardeners, too.

We now live on a farm, from which we hope we never have to move. But if it should ever happen that we'd need to pull up stakes, we'd be prepared to follow the guidelines that we've learned in our previous moves.

Before you move

1. Before listing the house for sale, divide perennial vegetables and flowers like rhubarb, iris, day lilies, phlox, and such, and plant each division in a clay pot or perforated can sunk in the ground.
2. Set aside a special nursery row for plant starts and divisions you intend to take with you to your new home, making it clear to prospective buyers of your house that this group of plants is not included in the sale.
3. Root cuttings of herbs, vines, houseplants, pussy willows, roses, grapevines, and other shrubby perennials either in the house or in your nursery row. (Dip the cut end in rooting hormone and insert it in damp vermiculite. Cover pot and stem with a plastic bag until roots form.) If you're planning your move a year in advance, you'll have time to root starts of shrubs like currant, flowering quince, boxwood, hazelnuts, and others. (Notch the underside of a young woody shoot, dust the bark wound with rooting hormone powder, bend it to the bare ground, and pat a clump of soil over it. Then put a rock on the branch to hold it in place.)
4. From February through April, you can take cuttings from fruit and nut trees. These cuttings, called scion wood, can be grafted to wild or inferior or seedling trees on your new place. Keep the cuttings cool and protect them from drying until you're ready to make the graft. To learn the technique, consult a good book on grafting available at your library, or see the bibliography at the back of this book for recommended reading.
5. Save seeds of all flowers and vegetables that form seed before you leave.
6. Start flats of early spring vegetables to plant in your new vegetable garden if distance is not too great.
7. Trees that have special sentimental value to you may, on occasion, be transplanted. New owners who have no interest in

certain trees that may be special to you will sometimes be willing to agree to a written exclusion of these plants from the agreement of sale. For your own protection, though, get the whole arrangement recorded and signed, no matter how amicable your verbal agreement may seem to be. (It is, of course, unfair to remove trees or shrubs which have been shown as part of the property and not specifically reserved, and illegal to do so if an agreement of sale has been signed.)

8. When you're offering your place for sale, take time to plant some bright quick-blooming flowers. A windowbox gay with geraniums and softly spilling vines, a cheerful accent of petunias or zinnias by the lamppost or mailbox, hollyhocks softening the garage wall – touches like these will make your home even more appealing.

9. I've made it a practice, when we move, to leave a diagram of the garden plantings for the new owner, naming fruit trees by variety and showing the location of spring bulbs that wouldn't be evident in the summer. Also, I usually start a small vegetable garden, both because I can't *help* planting something each spring, and because the food plants we've left behind have always seemed to mean a great deal to the new owners.

At your new home

1. Concentrate, the first year, on long-range improvements that will take time to show results, like the planting of fruit, nut, and ornamental trees and perennial vegetables. Soil-improving measures like manuring, composting, growing cover crops and green-manure crops will help the most if started early. (See *Vegetables Money Can't Buy.*)

2. Ask neighbors which plants do especially well or especially poorly in your area.

3. Treat yourself to an instant garden – a big flowerpot on the front step or a ring around the mailbox jammed with bright annual plants. Such a sign of home, a declaration of intent to put down roots, will do wonders for the morale of a family still stumbling over packing boxes and eating quick meals from mismatched plates.

   Moving has more than once given me a feeling of kinship with the pioneer woman who saved slips, seeds, and rooted cuttings from her old homestead to start anew in unfamiliar territory. For her it was a necessity. For us, retaining a favorite strain, an old family rose, an assortment of beloved perennials, a graft from a good fruit tree, has provided the sense of continuity that has made home wherever we've been.

It doesn't take long, in good deeply dug soil, for those transplants to put out roots and then to express their contentment by developing new crowns and shoots. Soon you'll be dividing them and sharing them with your new neighbors!

What's New in Garden Insect Control

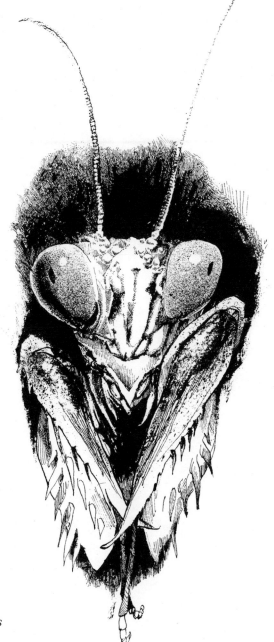

Preying Mantis

There is no garden without insects. Accustomed as we are to exercising nearly complete control over insect invasions of our homes, we may need to be reminded that it is not only unnecessary, but actually undesirable, for us to aim for anything approaching complete control of garden insects.

The web of life in the garden is incredibly complex. For each crop-threatening insect there is often at least one predator. Helpful predacious insects need a certain number of bad bugs to eat in order to stay alive. In many cases, predacious insects feed on specific bugs, or even on a single life-form – egg, larva, nymph, or adult – in the insect's life cycle. Soil, weather, plant health, variety in plant population, and bird activity also determine the kinds and numbers of insects that will be active in your garden.

The heavy-handed approach of treating food plants with wide-spectrum, long-lasting pesticides like Malathion, Sevin, Chlordane, and such wipes the slate clean for a while. Spraying your garden vegetables with Sevin will kill cucumber beetles, blister beetles, corn borers, bean beetles, potato beetles, and squash bugs. It will also kill the honeybees that pollinate the squash, cukes, and other crops, as well as many other innocuous and helpful insects. Worst of all, though, insects, with their brief life cycles, are able to adapt to chemical insults at an awesomely rapid rate, leaving you with a race of super bugs like those which have already made some chemical pesticides obsolete. In addition, valuable predacious insects decline when their prey has been wiped out and they have nothing to feed on.

Biological controls, increasingly studied by state agriculture stations and used by up-to-date farmers, orchardists, and gardeners, involve a more selective approach. With the study of insect feeding cycles and interrelationships has come a new respect for the exquisitely fragile balance of natural life-forms in the garden.

For example, on an aphid-infested rosebush inspected by entomologist Dr. William Jordan and described in his article 'Plant Pests and their Natural Enemies' in the January 1978 issue of *Horticulture,* syrphid flies, whose larvae eat young aphids, had deposited their eggs at precisely the right time and place to allow the coming larvae to take advantage of a new aphid hatch. Elsewhere on the same bush, Jordan spotted a lacewing fly larva puncturing and destroying the bodies of an adult aphid, and other aphids that had been killed by parasites. A quick hand on the spray can would have eliminated all of these effective, though slow-moving, controls.

What we need, it seems to me, is to accept a certain amount of insect damage, to recognize that we are dealing with a universe in miniature that has internal controls and interrelationships we've never dreamed of, to observe closely what goes on in our gardens, and to learn to identify insects, both the damaging and the helpful ones, so that we can determine when and how to interfere. Or whether to interfere at all. We garden activists often feel that we must have a solution for every problem, but sometimes it is better simply to wait and watch. Other natural forms will often bail you out.

For example, we usually have cabbage worms, the larvae of the white cabbage butterfly, on our cole crops. I often apply a spray solution of *Bacillus thuringiensis* which spreads a bacterial disease specific to caterpillars among the cabbage-eating larvae. This year, before I got the solution prepared, I noticed a nest of yellow jackets next to the cold frame near the garden. Yellow jackets prey on cabbage moth larvae. (Fortunately it was summer at the time and the cold frame wasn't the center of gardening activity that it had been earlier and would be later.) We accepted the nest. (What else could we do?) and were amazed to find that we had fewer cabbage worms that season than ever before. As is customary, the nest was abandoned in late summer, freeing the cold frame for my use in the fall. I almost hope the yellow jackets return next year.

Here's an adventure, then, that can last you all your life . . . learning to deal in a sane but effective way with your garden's insect enemies. New natural parasites, predators, and insect diseases are being discovered, and at the same time the time-honored measures of varying plant population and using traps and home-concocted sprays of resistant or aromatic plants are regaining respect as worthwhile options.

Bug Spray

One of the newest and most novel ways of killing undesirable insects was reported in *Organic Gardening and Farming* magazine as 'almost too good to be true.' If you find it difficult to believe that spraying a solution of ground-up insects will result in the death of many of the offending invaders, you probably have plenty of company. What interests me, though, is that gardeners are trying the method and finding that it works. First proposed by pest-control specialist Mike Sipe of Palmetto, Florida, and used successfully by some of his clients, this simple method of insect control involves collecting a handful of the undesirable bugs, liquefying them in the blender with a small amount of water and spraying the strained, diluted solution on the infested plants.

Why does it work? Sipe proposes several theories. It could be that bacteria or viruses infesting some of the insects are spread to insects sprayed by the solution, causing widespread disease in the ranks. Or, perhaps the odor of the ground-up bugs attracts their predators. It is also possible that distress pheromones (hormones produced by the insect's body in response to stress) somehow have an insect-repelling effect.

If you want to try to rout your garden's bad bugs by spraying them with their ground-up cousins, Sipe recommends the following procedure, as reported in Jeff Cox's article 'An Insect Control Method "Too Good To Be True"' in the October 1976 issue of *Organic Gardening and Farming:*

1. Collect a handful of insects. That is enough for even a large garden.
2. Identify the insect.
3. Avoid collecting insects that have parasites on them (like the large tomato hornworm hosting rice-grain-size ichneumon fly larvae on its back). They're already doomed and you don't want to kill the helpful parasites.
4. Buzz the insects in one cup of water in a blender. Amounts are not critical. If you can catch only a few bugs, use those. Sipe reports positive results with the use of as little as five cc. of bug juice in twenty-five gallons of water.
5. Strain out insect parts.
6. Dilute the solution with two cups of water to every one-quarter cup of concentrate.
7. Spray affected plants.
8. Record dates of treatment and results, if any.

Some gardeners have expressed concern over the handling and dissemination of insects affected by bacterial or viral diseases but USDA researcher Richard Ridgeway, quoted in 'The Bug Juice Method: How Safe? How Effective?' by Jeff Cox in the May 1977 issue of *Organic Gardening and Farming,* stated that most people who have worked with insect pathogens consider them safe to handle. Insect pathogens are apparently highly selective in their choice of a host. Naturally, one would wash one's hands after handling the bugs, and wash sprayed foods before eating them.

Insect-Plant Interaction

The coevolutionary nature of insect-plant interaction has only very recently been recognized. Plants defend themselves against insect attack much less passively than we had supposed. They have, in fact, evolved an amazing array of protective responses, all developed as defense strategies against insect attack: toxic compounds that make the plant inedible, substances like tannin that affect the growth rate of the predator, hormone-like compounds that interfere with normal maturation and development of the insect, and obvious physical impediments such as thorns, spines, and leaf hairs that impede movement or in some cases actually trap the insect.

Insects also change in response to plants. They learn to avoid the toxic plant and even develop resistance to plant toxins over the span of many generations. Then, of course, plants respond to new insect incursions by further refining their defense capabilities, producing new hormones or growing hairier leaves or developing a strong bitter taste.

Such is the coevolutionary process. It is continuous, and its implications are enormous. For if plants 'act,' over a period of time, rather than simply being acted upon, it should be possible to breed them for their content of certain hormones or other defensive agents, as well as to breed out plant-produced compounds that attract insects. Studies done by Dr. Lawrence B. Hendry and his team of researchers at the Pennsylvania State University, reported in 'Natural Insect Control 1975' by M. C. Goldman in the April 1975 issue of *Organic Gardening and Farming*, have revealed that sex lures formerly thought to be synthesized by female insects are in fact made by plants, eaten by the female insect, and stored in her body. Hendry suggests that it would be feasible to spray plants with a certain compound to imprint the insect larvae and later to treat the plants with the same chemical which would, at the proper time, constitute a sex lure that would throw the males off track and thus interfere with mating. In addition, the use of juvenile hormones isolated from plants to disrupt the insect's normal life cycle has produced encouraging results both in laboratory studies and field observations. Such controls, grounded in an understanding of real plant and insect behavior, make more sense than zapping all the life-forms in a field to eliminate a single troublesome one.

Far from being strictly academic, these studies will influence both plant varieties and management in the gardens of the future.

You can make use of these newly discovered plant and insect properties in your own garden, right now, by:

1. Saving seed of any non-hybrid plant that exhibits unusual resistance to insect attack. Who knows . . . it may be evolving more rapidly than the others.
2. Avoiding monoculture (large areas planted to a single kind of plant), which just makes things easy for the bugs. Variety confuses insects.
3. Trying companion planting. If aromatic pest-repellent plants like tansy, mint, garlic, basil, marigold, and such are spotted among the vegetable plantings, insect pests will be not only confused, but also, often, repelled, and in many cases the vegetables planted near them will thrive. Tomatoes, for example, are traditionally planted near the asparagus bed because their aromatic foliage repels the destructive asparagus beetle.
4. Observing and recording all you can about different planting plans you try and any positive or negative effects you notice.
5. Using plant-based sprays made by whirling hot peppers, garlic, tansy, tomato leaves, and other aromatic or repellent plants in the blender with two cups of water. Add a small amount of liquid soap to the strained solution and spray affected plants, making sure to hit the undersides of leaves as well as the tops.
6. Watching seed catalogs. One of the most important new directions in insect control is the breeding of pest-resistant plants. New strains of insect-resistant vegetables will probably be developed. Try them and evaluate their performance.
7. Rotating crops to avoid insect buildup.

Diseases, Parasites, and Predators

Attacking insects by introducing diseases, parasites, and predators is also a helpfully specific approach without side effects.

DISEASES

Diseases introduced to kill unwanted insects are highly specific and work quickly.

1. Bacillus thuringiensis (Brand names: Dipel, Biotrol, and
   Thuricide) affects insects that enter a caterpillar stage during
   their life cycle – the Lepidopterae. It is sold as a concentrated
   liquid, which should be diluted and sprayed on plants.
   Undersides of leaves should be sprayed because many pests hide
   there. The disease spores are soon killed by strong sun, so a
   cloudy day would be best for spraying. Timing is important
   here, too. Bacillus thuringiensis should be applied when
   caterpillars are present, since it doesn't affect eggs or adults.
   The disease paralyzes larvae in eighteen minutes and kills them
   in twelve hours. I have found it particularly useful against the
   larvae of the cabbage moth.
2. Milky spore disease kills the Japanese beetle, that imported
   scourge of the Eastern half of the United States. Available in a
   commercial preparation labeled 'Doom' or 'Japidemic,' the
   disease is spread by inoculating lawn areas, where the beetle
   grubs live, with the spore dust which has been obtained from
   grubs affected by milky spore disease. Expect to see results three
   years after applying the spores to your lawn; it takes that long
   for the disease to spread. If you can persuade your neighbors to
   treat their lawns too, you will all enjoy even more effective
   beetle control.

PARASITES

Here are two helpful parasites that can be introduced to home gardens:

1. Encarsia formosa. A miniscule wasp, which controls the
   whitefly infestations that are so common and troublesome in
   greenhouses and indoor plantings in the North, and on garden
   plants in the South.
       Encarsia adults are only ¹⁄₁₄₀ of an inch long, and most are
   females. Like aphids, they can reproduce without mating.
   Encarsia females lay eggs in the whitefly nymphs. They are
   capable of reducing whitefly populations by 80 to 90 percent. (If
   clouds of tiny white speck-sized moths fly out from under-leaf
   resting places when you work with your plants, they have
   whiteflies.)
       In releasing either predators or parasites in your garden,
   consider the initial release as a seeding, rather than as the final

answer. The first generation will multiply, and should continue to patrol your grounds all season long. An initial release of Vedalia beetles in Calfornia (see discussion of ladybugs) numbered only twenty-nine individuals, yet they multiplied and spread for miles. It is a good idea, also, to release insects in several small lots – say, every two weeks – rather than in a single large group. Ladybugs (see section on predators) are more likely to stay around if they have enough to eat, and small bunches of bugs are less likely to eat themselves out of business. Keep the reserved insects in a covered container in the refrigerator.

2. Trichogramma. Tiny wasps which destroy insect eggs . . . especially useful in controlling destructive caterpillars. Cards containing the minute trichogramma eggs are sold by firms dealing in biological controls. Correct timing is important. If the eggs you've distributed hatch and find no prey, the little wasps will die. Trichogramma eggs should be placed in the garden or orchard in time to hatch when the coddling moths are laying their eggs. Check with your county agricultural agent to find out when the moths usually begin egg laying in your area.

PREDATORS

Predators include:

1. Lacewing fly larvae *Chrysopa cubana*

The lacewing is a beautiful bug. Adults are one inch long with golden eyes and green wings that look as though they're overlaid with white lace. They emerge in spring when night temperatures are around 50 to 55 degrees F. Three to five generations are produced in a single season. The adult lifespan ranges from twenty to forty days. It is the lacewing larva, which hatches seven days after the egg is laid, that preys on garden pests like aphids, red spiders, and other mites. The rather grotesque looking larva, not unlike a miniature alligator in shape, grows from the size of an 'i' dot to one-fourth inch long by the end of its second week. While carrying debris (moss, aphid body husks, and so on) from its foraging on its back, it feeds voraciously on aphids, piercing their bodies with its sharp mouth parts and sucking out their body fluids after first injecting digestive enzymes to liquefy the aphid's organs and a tranquilizer to minimize struggling. Marvelous small-scale ferocity. Watch for lacewings in your garden and treat them gently. Introduced populations of lacewings will need at least two weeks to begin to make any inroads on the pest population.

2. Ladybugs *Hippodamia convergens*

Everyone likes ladybugs. These charming little black-spotted reddish beetles have enjoyed a good press, even in nursery rhymes. Both adults and larvae are death on aphids, mealy bugs, and scale insects. One variety, the Vedalia beetle, once saved the entire California citrus industry from a devastating infestation of cottony cushion scale. What many gardeners don't realize is that mail-order ladybugs will often migrate away from the area where you've released them, so you can't always be sure that they will do a great deal of good in *your* garden. They may end up spending most of their time down the road or on the other side of town, especially if they soon exhaust the aphid supply on your side of the fence.

Each ladybug that sticks around will eat fifty aphids a day. Even the larvae can consume a daily ration of twenty-five aphids apiece. An adult may lay as many as 1,500 eggs in a season. There are many kinds of ladybugs; Cynthia Westcott lists eight of the most common in *The Gardener's Bug Book*. Some have only two black spots, others lack spots, and some are black with red spots. Widespread spraying with DDT has decimated many ladybug populations. They are, however, fairly common in gardens. Two years ago we had an unusually large number of ladybugs in our garden. I was beginning to think that perhaps we were doing something right, but soon found out, after talking to many other local gardeners of all different persuasions, that apparently *everyone* had ladybugs that year. Perhaps the aphid crop was large. Ladybugs need a continuous supply of aphids to eat, and if every last pest disappears, they may starve unless they can find some scale or mealy bugs to tide them over.

3. Preying mantis *Tenodera aridifolia sinensis*

These members of the grasshopper order prey on a wide variety of other insects, both those that are garden pests and those that are helpful or harmless. They grasp their prey with their powerful front legs and will even strike at a hornet, frog, or lizard, according to plant doctor Cynthia Westcott. The young are born cannibals and begin to eat aphids and other small insects as soon as they are hatched. You will find the egg cases attached to branches of bushes and sturdy weeds. We often find them in our garden soybean and raspberry plantings. The egg cases are deposited in late summer or early fall but often become noticeable only when the leaves fall from the host plants. The cases are firm, dry, about the size and shape of your first thumb joint, and tan or gray in color, made of a frothy material containing many air cells. There are about 200 eggs in each case. If you buy mantis egg cases, tie them to the lower branches of a bushy shrub so that the young will have some protection when they hatch. If you buy cases in the fall, let them remain outdoors all winter. They are made to withstand the cold. If you bring them indoors, as I once did by mistake, the eggs may hatch early in the deceptively warm air. When I left an egg case on my kitchen desk, we soon had a kitchen full of hopping, wispy, nymph-like young . . . almost transparent but with the unmistakable long, lean-limbed look of their elders . . . all over the curtains, the houseplants, and dried weed arrangements. The cats thought we staged the event just for them. Luckily, it was warm outside at the time and we captured as many fragile young mantises as we could and scattered them around the garden.

Growth Regulation

Juvenile hormones are being used in some large-scale commercial food-growing operations. At least one such growth regulator is available for home garden use. Enstar 5F controls whitefly without affecting natural predators. Its effect is that of jamming normal progressive development. Treated whitefly eggs never hatch, and affected adults fail to reach sexual maturity.

The gardener's first line of defense remains the commonsense everyday practices that make for a healthy, well-balanced garden: building up the soil's humus content, rotating crops, planting a variety of different plant species close together, observing, wondering, experimenting, recording. Even if you never need or use any of these new insect control methods, simply looking closely, even minutely, at your garden plants and insects may lead you on a learning adventure of a different sort. And if you do have occasion to be exasperated by a particularly damaging insect invasion, check through this list of allies before considering a toxic spray that would kill helpful insects and help to breed a race of resistant harmful ones.

Bibliography

Abraham, George and Katy, 'Goodbye, White Fly,' *Organic Gardening and Farming*, November 1973, pp. 58–60.

Alsop, Gulielma. *April in the Branches*. New York: Dutton, 1947.

Anderson, Frederick O. *How to Grow Herbs for Gourmet Cooking*. New York: Meredith Press, 1967.

Bianco, Margery. *Green Grows the Garden*. New York: The Macmillan Co., 1936.

Brown, Edward Espe. *Tassajara Cooking*. Boulder, Col.: Shambala Publications, 1973.

Bubel, Nancy. *The Seed-Starter's Handbook*. Emmaus, Pa.: Rodale Press, 1978.

———. *Vegetables Money Can't Buy*. Boston: David R. Godine, 1977.

Cary, Mara. *Basic Baskets*. Boston: Houghton Mifflin, 1975.

Common Weeds of the United States, prepared by the Agricultural Service of the USDA. New York: Dover, 1971.

Cox, Jeff, 'The Bug Juice Method: How Safe? How Effective?' *Organic Gardening and Farming*, May 1977, pp. 164–172.

———. 'An Insect Control Method "Too Good to Be True",' *Organic Gardening and Farming*, October 1976, pp. 62–65.

Farb, Peter. *Living Earth*. New York: Harper and Bros., 1959.

Findhorn Community. *The Findhorn Garden*. New York: Harper & Row, 1975.

Gerard, John. *Gerard's Herball: The Essence Thereof Distilled by Marcus Woodward from the Editon of Dr. Johnson, 1636*. Totowa: N.J.: Minerva Press, 1975. (Reprint of 1927 edition.)

Gibbons, Euell. *Stalking the Healthful Herbs*. New York: David McKay, 1966.

———. *Stalking the Wild Asparagus*. New York: David McKay, 1962.

Goldman, M. C., 'Natural Insect Control 1975: Where It's at and Where It's Heading,' *Organic Gardening and Farming*, April 1975, pp. 82–92.

Greiner, T. *How to Make the Garden Pay*. Philadelphia: Wm. Henry Maule, 1894.

Harris, Gertrude. *Foods of the Frontier*. San Francisco: 101 Productions, 1972.

Hatfield, Audrey Wynne. *How to Enjoy Your Weeds*. New York: Sterling Publishing, 1973.

Herman, Matthias. *Herbs and Medicinal Flowers*. New York: Galahad Books, 1973.

Jordan, William, 'Plant Pests and Their Natural Enemies,' *Horticulture*, January 1978, pp. 27–31.

Kraft, Ken and Pat. *The Best of American Gardening*. New York: Walker and Co., 1975.

Llewellyn's Moon Sign Book, published annually by Llewellyn Publications, St. Paul, Minn. (1975 edition used).

Leighton, Ann. *Early American Gardens*. Boston: Houghton Mifflin, 1970.

LeQuenne, Fernand. *My Friend the Garden*. New York: Doubleday, 1965.

McCullough, David, 'The Backyard Gardens of Stouchsburg,' *Country Journal*, April 1977, pp. 34–40.

Miles, Bebe. *Bluebells and Bittersweet*. New York: Van Nostrand Reinhold, 1969.

Moffatt, Anne, 'How Plants Make War,' *Horticulture*, February 1978, pp. 39–45.

Nearing, Helen and Scott. *Living the Good Life*. New York: Galahad Books, 1970.

Parkinson, John. *A Garden of Pleasant Flowers: Paradisi in Sole Paradisus Terrestris*. New York: Dover, 1976. (Reprint of 1629 edition.)

Pellegrini, Angelo. *The Food-Lover's Garden*. New York: Alfred A. Knopf, 1970.

Raizen, Helen S., 'The Scientific Basis of Companion Planting as a Means of Insect Control,' *Organic Gardening and Farming*, May 1975, p. 45.

Raymond, Dick. *Down-to-Earth Vegetable Gardening*. Charlotte, Vt.: Garden Way, 1975.

Reppert, Bertha P. *A Heritage of Herbs*. Harrisburg, Pa.: Stackpole Books, 1976.

Rickett, Harold William. *Botany for Gardeners*. New York: The Macmillan Co., 1957.

Riotte, Louise. *Planetary Planting*. New York: Simon and Schuster, 1975.

Sackville-West, Vita. *A Joy of Gardening*. New York: Harper Bros., 1958.

Seeds, The Yearbook of Agriculture 1961, pp. 1–134; 288–294.

Simmonite, William, and Culpeper, Nicholas. *Herbal Remedies.* Hauppage, N.Y.: Award Books, 1977.

Sipe, Mike, 'Meet the Green Lacewing,' *Organic Gardening and Farming,* June 1977, pp. 144–148.

Smith, J. Russell. *Tree Crops.* New York: Devin-Adair, 1953.

Spencer, E. R. *Just Weeds.* New York: Charles Scribner's Sons, 1957.

Sperka, Marie. *Growing Wildflowers.* New York: Harper & Row, 1973.

Steffek, Edwin F. *Wild Flowers and How to Grow Them.* New York: Crown, 1954.

Sunset Pruning Handbook, by the Editors of Sunset Books. Menlo Park, Calif.: Lane Books, 1972.

Taylor, Kathryn S., and Hamblin, Stephen F. *Handbook of Wildflower Cultivation.* New York: The Macmillan Co., 1963.

Tiedjens, Victor A. *The Vegetable Encyclopedia.* New York: Avenel Books, 1943.

Tillona, Francesca, and Strowbridge, Cynthia. *A Feast of Flowers.* New York: Gramercy Publishing, 1969.

Tyler, Hamilton. *Gourmet Gardening.* New York: Van Nostrand Reinhold, 1972.

Weber, George G., and Ritter, Marshall T. *Propagating Nut Trees.* University Park, Pa.: The Pennsylvania State University, 1972.

Westcott, Cynthia. *The Gardener's Bug Book.* New York: Doubleday, 1973.

Wherry, Edgar T. *Wild Flower Guide.* New York: Doubleday, 1848.

Appendix A

PLANT SOCIETIES

American Fern Society, % Terry Lucansky, Department of Botany, University of Florida, Gainesville, Fla. 32601. Dues $5.00 a year.

American Hemerocallis Society, % Mrs. Arthur W. Parry, Signal Mountain, Tenn. 37377. Dues $7.50 a year.

American Horticultural Society, Mount Vernon, Va. 22121. Dues $15.00 a year.

American Primrose Society, % Mrs. Viskey Sauer, 1684 124th S.E., Renton, Wash. 98055. Dues $5.00 a year.

American Rock Garden Society, % William T. Hirsch, 3 Salisbury Lane, Malvern, Pa. 19355. Dues $7.50 a year.

New England Wildflower Society, % Ann Spence Dinsmore, Hemenway Road, Framingham, Mass. 01701. Dues $7.50 a year.

Northern Nut Growers Association, 4518 Holston Hills Road, Knoxville, Tenn. 37914. Dues $8.00 a year.

Appendix B

Sources of Supplies

(See appendix C for complete addresses of suppliers.)

Biological Controls
  Biological control sources based on information compiled by
  Organic Gardening and Farming magazine.

  Bacillus thuringiensis:
    Burpee
    William Dam
    Farmer
    Henry Field
    Gurney
    Jung
    Nichols
    Olds
  Encarsia:
    Greenhouse Bio Controls
    (Before ordering Encarsia, U.S. citizens must obtain a permit
    to import them for biological insect control from Technical
    Service Staff, PP&A APHIS USDA, Federal Center Building,
    Hyattsville, Md. 20782. Send this permit with your order.)
  Lacewing Fly:
    Bo-Bio-Control
    King Entomological Labs
    Rincon-Vitova Insectary
    World Garden Products
  Ladybugs:
    Bo-Bio-Control
    Burpee
    Lakeland
    Rincon-Vitova Insectary
    World Garden Products
  Milky Spore Disease:
    Fairfax Biological Laboratories
    Reuter Laboratories

Preying Mantis Egg Cases:
  Bo-Bio-Control
  Burpee
  Gurney
  King Entomological Labs
  World Garden Products
Trichogramma
  Bo-Bio-Control
  Rincon-Vitova Insectary
  Trik-O
  World Garden Products

Flowers

Perennial Garden Flower Seeds
Balloonflower:
  Comstock-Ferre
  DeGiorgi
  Park
Columbine:
  Burpee
  Olds
  Park
  R. H. Shumway
Day Lily:
  Burpee
  DeGiorgi
  Park
  R. H. Shumway
  Stokes
  Thompson and Morgan
Delphinium:
  Burpee
  Olds
  Park
  Stokes
Flax:
  Burpee
  Comstock-Ferre
  DeGiorgi
  Harris
  Olds
  Park

Primula:
  Burpee
  DeGiorgi
  Harris
  Olds
  Park
  Stokes
  Thompson and Morgan

Wildflower Seeds
Arbutus:
  American Rock Garden Society exchange list for members
  (see appendix A for address).
Black-eyed Susan:
  Clinebell
  Green Horizons
  Olds
  Clyde Robin
Bloodroot:
  Centennial Gardens
  Clyde Robin
Blue-eyed Grass:
  Clyde Robin
Bunchberry:
  Northplan
  Clyde Robin
Butterfly Weed:
  Clinebell
  Midwest
  Olds
  Clyde Robin
Cardinal Flower:
  Clinebell
  Midwest
  Clyde Robin
Columbine:
  Green Horizons
  Mellinger's
  Midwest
  Northplan
  Olds

Dogtooth Violet:
  DeGiorgi
  Midwest
  Northplan
  Park
  Thompson and Morgan
Forget-me-not:
  Mellinger's
  Olds
  Park
Gentian:
  Clinebell
  Mellinger's
  Midwest
  Park
  Clyde Robin
  Thompson and Morgan
Geranium (Wild):
  Mellinger's
  Midwest
  Olds
Hepatica:
  Midwest
Jack-in-the-Pulpit:
  DeGiorgi
Jacob's Ladder:
  DeGiorgi
  Midwest
  Thompson and Morgan
Lupine:
  Mellinger's
  Northplan
  Olds
  Clyde Robin
Mayapple:
  Thompson and Morgan
Shooting Star:
  Park
  Clyde Robin
  Thompson and Morgan

Solomon's Seal:
  Midwest
  Thompson and Morgan
Trillium:
  Midwest
  Park
  Thompson and Morgan
Virginia Bluebells:
  Midwest

Grapes
  Bountiful Ridge
  Burgess
  Farmer
  Henry Field
  Florida's Vineyard
  Dean Foster
  J. E. Miller
  Worley's

Herbs
  Hops:
    May (roots)
    Redwood City (seeds)
  Plants:
    Hemlock Hill
    Mellinger's
    Nichols
    Rosemary House
    The Yarb Patch
  Seeds:
    Appalachian Root and Herb Company
    Casa Yerba
    Otto Richter
    Yankee Peddler
    (Most general garden seed catalogs also carry herb seeds.)

Nutcracker
  Potter Walnut Cracker (for black walnuts, hickories, and so on)

Nut Trees
    Bountiful Ridge
    Burgess
    California Nursery Company
    Decorah Nursery
    Henry Field's
    Dean Foster
    Louis Geraldi Nursery
    Mellinger's
    J. E. Miller
    Worley's

Tea Plants
    Bee Balm:
        Grace's Gardens
        Midwest Wildflowers
        (See also herb dealers.)
    Chamomile:
        (See herb dealers.)
    Comfrey:
        Gurney
        Nichols
        North Central Comfrey Producers
    Elderberry:
        Burgess (plants)
        Dean Foster (plants)
        Gurney (plants)
        Redwood City (seeds)
        Clyde Robin (seeds)
        Zilke (plants)
    Lemon Verbena:
        (See herb dealers.)
    Linden Trees:
        Farmer (Redmond)
        Henry Field (Redmond and European)
        Earl May (*Tilia cordata var.*)

Vegetables
 Asparagus:
  (Most seed catalogs carry asparagus seed.)
 Beans, Heirloom:
  Vermont Bean Seed Company
 Burdock:
  Gurney
  Hudson
  Johnny's
  Kitazawa
  Nichols
  Redwood City
 Cardoon:
  DeGiorgi
  Comstock-Ferre
  William Dam
  Gurney
  Hudson
  Le Jardin
  Nichols
  Redwood City
 Chayote:
  Reuter Seed Company
 Chinese Cabbage:
  Johnny's
  Kitazawa
  Thompson and Morgan
  Tsang and Ma
 Chinese Celery (Heung Kuhn):
  Mellinger's
  Thompson and Morgan
  Tsang and Ma
 Corn Salad:
  DeGiorgi
  Harris
  Le Jardin
  Nichols
  R. H. Shumway
 Gai Choy (Chinese Mustard):
  Kitazawa
  Mellinger's
  Redwood City
  Tsang and Ma

Gai Lohn (Chinese Broccoli):
  Grace's Gardens
  Redwood City
  Tsang and Ma
Globe Artichoke:
  Burpee
  DeGiorgi
  Hudson
  Morgan
  Thompson
Gow Choy (Chinese Chives):
  Grace's Gardens
  Le Jardin
  Mellinger's
  Nichols
  Thompson and Morgan
  Tsang and Ma
Hinn Choy (Chinese Spinach):
  Mellinger's
  Tsang and Ma
Mao Gwa (Chinese Fuzzy Gourd):
  Mellinger's
  Tsang and Ma
Martynia:
  DeGiorgi
  Park
  Redwood City
  R. H. Shumway
Rocket:
  Burpee
  Comstock-Ferre
  DeGiorgi
  Gurney
  Hudson
  Le Jardin
  Nichols
  Park
  Redwood City
Savoy Spinach (Cold-Resistant):
  Burpee (variety 'Winter Bloomsdale')
  Stokes

Scorzonera:
  DeGiorgi
  Hudson
  Johnny's
  Le Jardin
  Thompson and Morgan
Shungiku:
  Hudson
  Johnny's
  Kitazawa
  Park
  Redwood City
  Thompson and Morgan
Skirret:
  Hemlock Hill Herb Farm (plants)
Sorrel:
  Comstock-Ferre
  Redwood City
Watercress:
  Burpee
  Centennial Gardens
  William Dam

Appendix C

Addresses of Suppliers

Abundant Life Seed Foundation, Box 30018, Seattle, Wash. 98103. Catalog $1.00.

Appalachian Root and Herb company, 37 Center Street, Rainelle, W. Va. 25962.

Bo-Bio-Control, Inc., 54 South Bear Creek Drive, Merced, Calif. 95340.

Bountiful Ridge Nurseries, Inc., Princess Anne, Md. 21853.

Burgess Seed and Plant Company, P.O. Box 3000, Galesburg, Mich. 49053.

Burpee Seeds, Warminster, Pa. 18974; also Clinton, Iowa 52732; and Riverside, Calif. 92501.

California Nursery Company, Box 2278, Fremont, Calif. 94536.

Casa Yerba, Star Route 2, Box 21, Days Creek, Ore. 97429.

Centennial Gardens, Box 4516, M.P.O., Vancouver, Canada V6B 3Z8. Rare and unusual seeds.

Richard Clinebell, Native Plants, 3865 21st Street, San Francisco, Calif. 94114. Seed list $1.00.

Comstock-Ferre, 263 Main Street, Wethersfield, Conn. 06109.

William Dam Seeds, West Flamboro, Ontario, Canada LOR 2KO.

Decorah Nursery, 504 Center Avenue, Decorah, Iowa 52101.

DeGiorgi Company, Council Bluffs, Iowa 51501. Catalog 50¢.

Fairfax Biological Laboratories, Clinton Corners, N.Y. 12514.

Farmer Seed and Nursery Company, Faribault, Minn. 55201.

Henry Field's, Shenandoah, Iowa 51602.

Florida's Vineyard Nursery, Box 300, Orange Lake, Fla. 32681.

Dean Foster Nurseries, Hartford, Mich. 49057.

Louis Geraldi Nursery, Route 1, O'Fallon, Ill. 62269.

Grace's Gardens, 22 Autumn Lane, Hackettstown, N.J. 07840. Catalog 25¢.

Green Horizons Wildflowers, 500 Thompson, Kerrville, Tex. 78028.

Greenhouse Bio Controls, 61 Horvath Street, Kingsville, Ontario, Canada.

Gurney Seed and Nursery Company, Yankton, S.D. 57078.

Harris Seeds, Moreton Farms, Rochester, N.Y. 14624.

Charles Hart Seed Company, 304 Main Street, Wethersfield, Conn. 06109.

Hemlock Hill Herb Farm, Litchfield, Conn. 06759. Catalog 50¢.

J. L. Hudson, Seedsman, P.O. Box 1058, Redwood City, Calif. 94064. Catalog 50¢.

Johnny's Selected Seeds, Albion, Maine 04910. Catalog 50¢.

J. W. Jung Seed Company, Randolph, Wis. 53956.

King Entomological Labs, P.O. Box 69, Limerick, Pa. 19468.

Kitazawa Seed Company, 356 West Taylor Street, San Jose, Calif. 95110.

Lakeland Nurseries, Hanover, Pa. 17331.

Le Jardin du Gourmet, Box 5, Route 15, West Danville, Vt. 05873. Catalog 50¢.

May Nursery, 2215 W. Lincoln, Box 1312, Yakima, Wash. 98907.

Earl May Seed and Nursery Company, Shenandoah, Iowa 51603.

Mellinger's, 2310 West South Range, North Lima, Ohio 44452. Stamps appreciated for catalog.

Midwest Wildflowers, Box 64, Rockton, Ill. 61072. Catalog 50¢.

J. E. Miller Nurseries, Inc., Canandaigua, N.Y. 14424.

Nichols Garden Nursery, 1190 North Pacific Highway, Albany, Ore. 97321. Catalog 25¢.

North Central Comfrey Producers, Box 195, Glidden, Wis. 54527.

Northplan Seed Producers, P.O. Box 9107, Moscow, Idaho 83843.

Olds Seed Company, P.O. Box 1969, Madison, Wis. 53701.

Park Seed Company, Greenwood, S.C. 29647.

Potter Walnut Cracker, Box 930, Sapulpa, Okla. 74066.

Redwood City Seed Company, P.O. Box 361, Redwood City, Calif. 94064.

Reuter Laboratories, 2400 James Madison Highway, Haymarket, Va. 22069.

Reuter Seed Company, Inc., New Orleans, La. 70179.

Otto Richter and Sons Ltd., Box 26, Goodwood, Ontario, Canada LOC 1AO. Catalog 50¢.

Rincon-Vitova Insectary, Inc., P.O. Box 95, Oak View, Calif. 93022.

Clyde Robin Seed Company, P.O. Box 2855, Castro Valley, Calif. 94546. Wildflowers. Catalog $1.00.

Rosemary House, 120 South Market Street, Mechanicsburg, Pa. 17055. Catalog 50¢.

Sanctuary Seeds, 1913 Yew Street, Vancouver, British Columbia, Canada V6K 3G3.

R. H. Shumway, Seedsman, Rockford, Ill. 61101.

Stokes Seeds, Inc., P.O. Box 548, Buffalo, N.Y. 14240; also Stokes
    Seeds Ltd., St. Catherine's, Ontario, Canada L2R 6R6.
Thompson and Morgan, Inc., P.O. Box 100, Farmingdale, N.J.
    07727; also % Canadian Garden Products Ltd., 132 James
    Avenue East, Winnipeg, Manitoba, Canada R3B ON8.
Trik-O, Gothard, Inc., P.O. Box 370, Canutillo, Tex. 79835.
Tsang and Ma International, 1556 Laurel Street, San Carlos, Calif.
    94070.
Vesey's Seeds Ltd., York, Prince Edward Island, Canada COA 1 PO.
Vermont Bean Seed Company, Garden Lane, Bomoseen, Vt. 05732.
Wanigan Associates, 262 Salem Street, Lynnfield, Mass. 01940.
    Some seeds free with $5.00 membership.
World Garden Products, 2 First Street, East Norwalk, Conn. 06855.
Worley's Nurseries, Route 1, York Springs, Pa. 17372.
Yankee Peddler Herb Farm, Highway 36N, Brenham, Tex. 77833.
    Plants and seeds. Catalog $1.00.
The Yarb Patch, 3726 Thomasville Road, Tallahassee, Fla. 32303.
    Catalog 25¢.
Zilke, Baroda, Mich. 49101.

Index

THE ADVENTUROUS GARDENER *was designed by Richard Hendel, with illustrations by Barry Moser. The book was typeset by Dix Typesetting Co. Inc. in VIP Trump Mediaeval, a typeface created by Professor George Trump in 1954 and originally cast by C. E. Weber Foundry in Germany. The face is known for its wedge-shaped serifs, its narrow capital letters, and its calligraphic style.*